WHO JESUS AIN'T

Introducing Jesus of Nazareth

By
Steve DiSebastian

Who Jesus Ain't

Some sections of this book have appeared
in one form or another on the blog
God From the Machine Blog

God From the Machine blog: godfromthemachineblog.wordpress.com

Follow *God From the Machine* on Facebook:
Facebook.com/godfromthemachine.blog

Follow Steve DiSebastian on Twitter: @SteveDiSeb

Point Community Church: pointcommunitychurch.org

Table of Contents

Who Jesus Ain't

Dedicated to

Avery

The first of the new generation of our family
The first with fiery hair
The first of the new generation baptized
in the name of the Father, the Son, and the Holy Spirit

Now there are also many other things that Jesus did. Were every one of them to be written, I suppose that the world itself could not contain the books that would be written.

John 21:25

INTRODUCTION: JESUS AIN'T A WHITE GUY

Jesus of Nazareth wasn't a white guy.

The vast majority of what we know about Jesus comes from the New Testament. Whether someone believes the New Testament is the Word of God or not, doesn't change this fact (but more about that later). And based on the New Testament record, other history, and plain ol' logic, we know Jesus ain't a white guy.

OK, let's be clear: We have no idea what Jesus looked like, including the complexion of his skin. Nothing in the New Testament or anywhere else describes him as tall, dark, and handsome or fair-skinned, pale, or pasty. But we know for sure he wasn't European.

Who Jesus Ain't

Jesus was a Jew from Palestine, the region east of the Mediterranean Sea, a relatively thin strip of land between the sea and the Jordan River. Since people who come from that part of the world tend to have darker skin and hair, we can be fairly certain that many of those paintings we grew up seeing of Jesus looking like some fair-skinned, light-haired and blue-eyed first century heart-throb are inaccurate.

In fact, the only other clue that I know of that gives us any idea about Jesus' appearance comes from a book in the Old Testament written 700 years before Jesus' life. The prophet Isaiah wrote about someone often referred to as the "Suffering Servant," which was interpreted before the time of Jesus as the coming Messiah, the Jewish king who would lead Israel to victory.

Isaiah wrote,

For he grew up before him like a young plant,
and like a root out of dry ground;
he had no form or majesty that we should look at him,
and no beauty that we should desire him.
He was despised and rejected by men;
a man of sorrows, and acquainted with grief;
and as one from whom men hide their faces
he was despised, and we esteemed him not. (Isaiah 53:2-3)

Isaiah 53 goes on to describe how the Suffering Servant will undeservedly suffer and die for the sins of others, yet he will *"make many to be accounted righteous."*[1] Anyone familiar with the Christian belief that Jesus of Nazareth died for the sins of the world can easily see why so many have understood this prophecy to be about Jesus.

It's interesting to note that Isaiah writes that Jesus had *"no form or majesty that we should look at him, and no beauty that we should*

---

[1] Isaiah 53:11.
[2] Matthew 16:13-20; Mark 8:27-30; Luke 9:18-20.

desire him. Is this referring only to Jesus' humble life, that there was nothing kingly or ornate about him? Or do these verses tell us that nothing about Jesus' physical appearance was overly impressive or attractive either?

I lean towards thinking that both understandings are correct. Jesus didn't live a life of majesty as a king, and I also think Jesus simply looked like a regular dude. He looked like a typical guy for the time period and region of the world he lived in. He wasn't ugly, but he wasn't handsome. He was the sort of guy that wouldn't catch your attention in a crowd. Could I be wrong? Certainly. But I can at least tell you *this* with confidence: Jesus ain't a white guy. Or an Asian guy. Or an African guy.

Sometimes it's easier to say what Jesus ain't rather than what he is.

The Question

In three of the four Gospels written about Jesus of Nazareth found in the New Testament, we're told about a conversation between Jesus and his original twelve disciples.[2] Jesus asks, ***"Who do people say that I am?"*** The disciples give several answers: John the Baptist, Elijah, Jeremiah, or another one of the Old Testament prophets returned. Then Jesus asks them this:

"But who do YOU say that I am?"

Jesus knew how to use questions to bring an important issue into the light. This question may be the most important question ever asked, because if Jesus is who he says he is, then how you answer that question will have a profound effect on your life and beyond.

---

[2] Matthew 16:13-20; Mark 8:27-30; Luke 9:18-20.

Who Jesus Ain't

Throughout history, people have answered Jesus' question in many ways, and this carries over to this very day. Everyone has an opinion about who Jesus is.

Secular culture says Jesus was just a wise, good man – a moral teacher – but not divine. Quite the opposite, not long after Christianity's beginning, followers of the heresies of Docetism and Gnosticism taught that Jesus was completely spirit and only seemed to be human. Others in modern secular culture proclaim Jesus never existed at all – that he's a myth or legend. Meanwhile, Jim Jones, David Koresh, "Christ" Ahnsahnghong, and other modern cult leaders have claimed to be Jesus himself returned to the earth!

Protestant Christians and Roman Catholics both believe Jesus was completely God and man, but Roman Catholics believe his death on the cross alone was not sufficient for salvation. Muslims believe Jesus was born of a virgin, performed miracles, lived a sinless life, and he'll return on Judgment Day, but he didn't die on a cross, and he's not God in the flesh, but only a prophet. Those in the New Age movement make Jesus out to be an enlightened being, not much different than Buddha. Mormons claim Jesus is the firstborn spirit child of God, who used to be a man, and Lucifer is Jesus' spirit brother. Jehovah's Witnesses say Jesus is not God, but a created being lower than God but higher than angels.

Many paintings portray Jesus with the complexion, hair, and facial features of whatever region of the world produced the artwork, whether European, Asian, Indian, or African. Some paintings make Jesus look like a hippy. A popular T-shirt in the early 2000s announced "Jesus is my homeboy." Some make Jesus out to be liberal, while others make him out as conservative – either politically or theologically. Writers have tried to argue that Jesus was an apocalyptic prophet or an armed revolutionary or even a traveling Buddhist monk.

Who Jesus Ain't

How would you answer Jesus' question? Who do you say Jesus of Nazareth is?

I hope this book will help you answer that question because it may be the most important question you ever answer.

CHAPTER 1: JESUS AIN'T BORN TO PRIVILEGE

A King But Not Born a King

Jesus is a descendant of Abraham, the father of the Israelite (Jewish) nation, and King David. His parents were from Nazareth in Galilee, and he was raised there, but he was born in Bethlehem, the city of David. This is important because Old Testament passages understood to be about the coming Messiah say he will be a descendant of King David and he will come from Bethlehem.

You have said, "I have made a covenant with my chosen one;
I have sworn to David my servant:
'I will establish your offspring forever,

and build your throne for all generations.'"
(Psalm 89:3-4)

But you, O Bethlehem Ephrathah,
who are too little to be among the clans of Judah,
from you shall come forth for me
one who is to be ruler in Israel,
whose coming forth is from of old,
from ancient days.
Therefore he shall give them up until the time
when she who is in labor has given birth;
then the rest of his brothers shall return
to the people of Israel.
And he shall stand and shepherd his flock in the strength of the Lord,
in the majesty of the name of the LORD his God.
And they shall dwell secure, for now he shall be great
to the ends of the earth.
And he shall be their peace. (Micah 5:2-5)

This understanding of the Old Testament prophecies about the future deliverer of the Jews is seen in the birth narrative of the Gospel of Matthew when the magi (non-Jewish wise men), seeing a sign in the stars, come to Jerusalem asking where to find the King of the Jews. Herod the Great, ruler of Judea but not a descendant of King David nor a true king, gathers the chief priests and scribes and asks them where the Messiah will be born. They answer, *"In Bethlehem in Judea, for so it is written in the prophet"* and they quote the passage from Micah 5.[3]

This is also seen in the Gospel of John:

When they heard these words [of Jesus'], some of the people said, "This really is the Prophet." Others said, "This is the Christ."[4] But some said,

---

[3] Matthew 2:5-6.
[4] "Christ" (Greek) = "Messiah" (Hebrew).

"Is the Christ to come from Galilee? Has not the Scripture said that the Christ comes from the offspring of David, and comes from Bethlehem, the village where David was?" (John 4:40-42)

Both the Gospel of Matthew and Luke report that Mary, Jesus' mother, was a virgin and Jesus' conception was a miracle from God through the Holy Spirit. So, Jesus, "the Son of God" – as Gabriel (the angel who brings Mary this news) calls him[5] – is not a blood relation to his earthly father, Joseph.

The angel tells Mary,

He will be great and will be called the Son of the Most High. And the Lord God will give to him the throne of his father David, and he will reign over the house of Jacob forever, and of his kingdom there will be no end." (Luke 1:32-33)

He also tells Mary to name her son Jesus, which means "God saves."

How Can You Divorce Someone You're Not Married To?

Understandably, confusion comes when someone today reads in Matthew that Mary's *"husband Joseph, being a just man and unwilling to put her to shame, resolved to divorce her quietly"* when he learned she was pregnant.[6] So, was Mary an unmarried virgin or not? Why is Joseph her "husband" but they don't seem to be married? And if they're not married, how do you divorce someone you're not married to?

This misunderstanding has to do with our modern, western understanding of engagement and marriage versus the culture of Mary

---

[5] Luke 1:35.
[6] Matthew 1:19.

and Joseph. Simply, once a marriage was arranged in Mary's day, though the couple may not be living together or fully married through a ceremony, it was still a binding relationship in a legal sense. So, where in our culture marriage engagements that are broken lead to a lot of hard feelings, a broken engagement in Mary and Joseph's day would have an added legal aspect to it, so Joseph planned to "divorce" her.

Fortunately, an angel of the Lord appeared to Joseph in a dream and, as we can guess, left quite an impression because Joseph married Mary. This angel told Joseph, as it was done with Mary, to call the child Jesus – "God saves."

What Was Life Like for Mary & Joseph?

The New Testament for the most part doesn't report what life was like for Mary and Joseph immediately after their marriage. The wording of **Matthew 1:18-19** (*"she was found to be with child"*) suggests that perhaps others learned of Mary's pregnancy before she married Joseph. We have no record of whether she spoke to Joseph about it first or if he found out through others.

After their marriage, were they treated like outcasts? Was Joseph belittled for marrying a woman who was pregnant before marriage? Did Jesus grow up with the stigma of being a child conceived out of wedlock?

Interestingly, in **John 8**, John records a debate between Jesus and some religious leaders. We don't need to unpack the whole debate here, but it's a debate about fatherhood, whether those in the debate are children of Abraham and God or of Satan. In **John 8:41**, one of the religious leaders abruptly retorts, *"**We were not born of fornication**"*[7] (or "of sexual immorality"). New Testament scholar D.A. Carson writes in his

---

[7] John 8:41.

commentary on the Gospel of John[8] that this may be a cheap shot (my words) at Jesus by his opponents. Mark Strauss in his book *Four Portraits, One Jesus* mentions this interpretation as well.[9] It's possible the religious leaders in Jerusalem, after looking into this man who is raising so many eyebrows, learned of the questionable situation surrounding his birth. There is no further evidence for this view, but it's interesting to contemplate nonetheless, and it definitely seems like an odd comment for the religious leaders to throw in during the debate.

No Room at the Inn – Another Clue?

Perhaps one of the most famous images of the birth of Jesus comes from only one sentence in the entire Bible:

And she gave birth to her firstborn son and wrapped him in swaddling cloths and laid him in a manger, because there was no place for them in the inn. (Luke 2:7)

Even non-Christians are familiar with the iconic nativity scenes at Christmas: the newborn Jesus laying on hay in a manger, surrounded by farm animals in a barn. The thing is, the word for "inn" (*katalyma*) in the original ancient Greek normally means a guest room in a home or an informal public shelter where travelers (such as in caravans) would stay for the night. Luke uses a different word for a roadside inn (*pandocheion*) later in 10:34, so it seems unlikely that he would use a different word if he meant the same thing.

Further, Luke 2:7 only speaks of the newborn Jesus being laid in a manger; it doesn't tell us where that manger is located. It could very

---

[8] *The Gospel of John* (Pillar New Testament Commentary) by D.A. Carson (APOLLOS, 1991).
[9] *Four Portraits, One Jesus: A Survey of Jesus and the Gospels* by Mark L. Strauss (Zondervan, 2007).

well be a lower-level stall attached to the home of a relative of Joseph or even a cave, as some traditions suggest. People used natural and man-made caves in the many slopes around Bethlehem as a cost-effective way to provide shelter for farm animals.

So, I hope this doesn't ruin anyone's fond Christmas memories, but those classic nativity scenes we all love may be inaccurate.

Because of the census, Joseph and Mary were away from home at the time of Jesus' birth since Joseph had to register in Bethlehem. Many people must have been traveling for the census, so it's understandable that the "inn" had "no room." But I've always had a hard time imagining how the people in the inn (whether it be a guest room, public shelter, or even a roadside inn) could turn away an extremely pregnant woman. Could this be further evidence of poor treatment of Mary and Joseph because of Mary being perceived as an immoral harlot? If the "inn" is, in fact, a guest room in the home of a family member of Joseph, it gives this idea more plausibility. It's logical to assume that Joseph had relatives in his hometown. Did they turn their back on Joseph for marrying such a woman?

Or perhaps Joseph and Mary simply saw the crowded conditions of the guest room or public shelter and found more comfort in an area for animals. People in the first century often lived in close proximity to their livestock. **Luke 2:7** simply says, *"...because there was no room for them in the inn."* It doesn't say Joseph and Mary were refused, unwelcomed, or even kicked-out, though I have a hard time imagining a scene where Joseph and Mary arrive at a family member's home, find the guest room overcrowded, and decide to stay with the animals instead, and the rest of the family is okay with this: "Sounds like a great idea! Let the pregnant lady give birth with the animals!"

Or perhaps it was discrimination of some other sort. We're told Joseph was a carpenter. (The word translated "carpenter" – *tekton* – is a general term for someone who works with stone, wood, or metal.) Most likely, scholars say, he would've been a part of the "working poor." The best biblical support that shows Mary and Joseph's relative poverty is in **Luke 2:24** when Mary offers at the Temple a sacrifice of two doves and two pigeons, which is said in the Old Testament[10] to be an acceptable sacrifice for the poor if they can't afford a lamb.

Finally, Nathanael's sarcastic response when Philip first tells him about Jesus might give us another clue:

Philip found Nathanael and said to him, "We have found him of whom Moses in the Law and also the prophets wrote, Jesus of Nazareth, the son of Joseph." Nathanael said to him, "Can anything good come out of Nazareth?" (John 1:45-46)

Conclusions VS. Assumptions

Now, notice: some of what I said above was citing evidence from the Bible, and other things I said were my ideas based on looking at that written evidence. This is something one does continually as an English major: you read, draw conclusions, defend your conclusions, repeat. In seminary, you do much of the same thing – but while reading the Bible of course.

Some conclusions are better than others, and that usually depends on the quality or quantity of the evidence supporting that opinion. Some conclusions aren't even really conclusions because they're hardly based on evidence (if any)! This is *speculation*. A lot of things people say about Jesus are speculation, not logical, evidence-based conclusions.

Please weigh any ideas I present in this book against the evidence. And don't just look at the evidence I present to you in here. Open the Bible and look at the evidence yourself *in context*; do some research. Above, I

---

[10] Leviticus 12:8.

draw some conclusions about the social status of Mary, Joseph, and Jesus, and some of my conclusions may even be considered speculation. Feel free to ignore any or all of the conclusions or speculations I draw in this book, but don't disregard the evidence. The evidence is what's most important. So, the big question now is: Can we trust the evidence? We'll explore this question more in Chapter 3, but first let's talk more about Christmas.

CHAPTER 2: JESUS AIN'T BORN ON DECEMBER 25th

It's easy to remember (approximately) how long ago Jesus of Nazareth was born (and when we're talking about ancient history, mostly everything is "approximate") because our western dating system is centered around his birth. Thus, just over 2,000 years ago, Jesus was born in Bethlehem.

The Gospels of Matthew and Luke, the only two Gospels to give us the birth narratives of Jesus, don't tell us the date Jesus was born, but they do tell us Caesar Augustus and Herod the Great were in power. Ancient historians often "date" the events they're writing about by telling who was in power. Most scholars put Jesus' birth somewhere between 7 BC and 4 BC. A sixth-century monk named Dionysius Exiguus developed our modern calendar, but it appears he miscalculated the birth of Jesus by at least four years. Furthermore, as far as the actual month and day of Jesus' birth, no one knows. As stated above, the Bible doesn't say.

The earliest known date Christians celebrated Christmas was January 6th, and some churches in the east still do so today. Celebrating on December 25th appears, as some have theorized, to have started during the reign of Roman Emperor Constantine over 300 years after Jesus' birth. The day was likely the pagan "holiday" of Saturnalia and instead of simply banning these ceremonies, Constantine (the first emperor to become Christian) may have changed it to a Christian celebration to help ease his empire from paganism to Christianity.

A similar theory points out that the winter solstice is very close to December 25th, and another theory says December 25th is when Emperor Aurelian dedicated his temple to the god Sol Invictus. Constantine, before becoming Christian, had worshipped Sol Invictus and, thus, picked this date to instead celebrate Christmas.[11]

On the other hand, Gregg Allison, Professor of Christian Theology at Southern Baptist Theological Seminary and author of *Historical Theology: An Introduction to Christian Doctrine*, doesn't think these theories are plausible. He says the church in the 3rd and 4th centuries were certainly not open to pagan practices. In fact, at that time the church "denounced any association with paganism and pagan festivals." Allison goes on to explain that the early church believed Jesus was conceived on the same day he was crucified. (Why? No one knows for certain anymore, perhaps because they just liked the symmetry.) This would put Jesus' conception during the Passover, which would've

---

[11] Much of the information in this section is from *Four Portraits, One Jesus: A Survey of Jesus and the Gospels* by Mark L. Strauss and *The Case For the Real Jesus* by Lee Strobel.

been the 14th or 15th of Nisan on the Jewish calendar. That would be March 25th on the Roman calendar for Jesus' conception through the Holy Spirit, and then nine months later is – you guessed it – December 25th.[12]

What About the 3 Wise Men?

How many wise men visited the newborn Jesus on the first Christmas? Was it three? Or was it not three wise men, but three kings?

The Gospel of Matthew only says that the magi – non-Jewish wise men *"from the east"* – arrived "after Jesus was born."[13] Most likely, the magi were pagan priests who studied astrology. No mention of any kings visiting the young Jesus is recorded in the New Testament.

During their search to find this new king, the magi stopped in Jerusalem. King Herod, learning from the magi of the birth of this new king of the Jews, asked the magi to inform him when they find the new king so he could also honor him, though Herod secretly planned to kill him. The Jewish chief priests and scribes told the magi that, according to Scripture, the Messiah would be born in Bethlehem, so it logically follows that the magi would go there next. Warned in a dream not to return to Herod, the magi return to their home country *"by another way"* after visiting Jesus.

Learning that the magi had tricked him, Herod orders all boys ages *two and younger* in Bethlehem and the surrounding area killed. Earlier, Herod had questioned the magi about the exact time when the star that had brought them searching for the new king of the Jews had appeared. So, when the magi arrived, it's possible Jesus was around two-years-old. When the magi find him, Jesus is described as a "child," which could be

---

[12] *Southern Seminary Magazine*, Spring 2012, Volume 80, Number 2.
[13] Matthew 2:1.

a baby or an older child. Keep in mind, the magi didn't have modern transportation and we don't know from how far away they traveled.[14]

History definitely supports the idea that Herod was capable of doing such a horrible thing. Herod was not even technically a Jew, and the Romans had placed him in power. He was seen as a traitor and a sell-out to most Jews. Herod was so protective of his power that he killed his own wife, some of his sons, and many rabbis, who he saw as threats.

If Jesus was two years old when the magi arrived, does this mean after Jesus' birth, Joseph and Mary stayed in Bethlehem for an extended time (possibly with family)? How much time lapsed between when the magi first saw the star and they arrived in Bethlehem? After all, they saw the child Jesus in a "house."[15] Or is this another clue that maybe Jesus wasn't born in a barn or cave, though he was laid in a manger after his birth?

Also, Matthew doesn't report how many magi came. The tradition of three magi traveling to find Jesus likely comes from the three types of gifts brought by them to the child king: gold,[16] frankincense, and myrrh. The Christmas song "We Three Kings" confuses things even more! Further, nothing in the Gospels explicitly states Jesus was born during the day or night.

---

[14] See Matthew 2.

[15] Matthew 2:11.

[16] Some have asked: *So, what happened to the gold?* First, the evidence seems clear that Joseph and Mary were relatively poor and Jesus grew up as a humble carpenter's son. Secondly, some have suggested that this gold allowed Mary and Joseph to flee to safety in Egypt to escape from Herod's slaughter of the children (See Matthew 2). This is an interesting idea and, I think, a reasonable speculation – though a speculation just the same. Lastly, remember, there is much more we *don't* know about Jesus' life before his ministry than what we *do* know. We simply don't know how much gold was given or what financial hardships Jesus' family faced before he started his ministry.

Who Jesus Ain't

I'll have to say, the most plain, straightforward reading of the account in Matthew supports the traditional interpretation that the magi arrived in Bethlehem sometime near the time of Jesus' birth. The fact that they followed a star implies they did arrive at night. Further, we're also told an angel appeared to the shepherds as they were watching their flocks by night, which further implies Jesus was born at night.[17]

But it's a good exercise to read the Bible closely and consider these possibilities. We grow so used to hearing or seeing many of the narratives in the Bible portrayed certain ways – especially the most popular stories of the Bible, and definitely something as widely known and adapted as the Christmas story – it's good for us to take a close look at the source, see what it truly says, and imagine the story for ourselves. Doing so will bring to life passages that we may have taken for granted for a long time, and it may lead us to seeing something new that we have overlooked dozens of times before.

---

[17] From what we know about the culture, it's also much more likely that the shepherds were not middle-aged men, but middle-school-aged boys and even girls.

CHAPTER 3: JESUS AIN'T UNDOCUMENTED

It seems everyone has an opinion about Jesus. Some say he was a wise, moral man; some say he was a myth; some say he was God in the flesh.

But first, how do we even know about Jesus? This seems like a pretty basic question, but before we can answer who Jesus *ain't*, we need to understand how we know about him in the first place.

We learn about specific people in the past by documentation, by records that bear witness to that person's life, and sometimes other archaeological evidence. Obviously, the farther back in history we go, the more difficult it is to prove the existence of a particular person, even someone as famous and powerful as a king or emperor, let alone a poor rabbi from the backwaters of the Roman empire.

So, why is it so hard to conclusively prove the existence of a person from ancient times, even someone as famous and influential as Alexander the Great or Caesar Augustus? First, empirical science is little help. Even if we had the assumed body of the ancient person, it's not like there's a DNA database we can reference.

Further, there are two types of science: *empirical* and *forensic*. Empirical science is used to study present, repeatable events. These events can be replicated in studies and witnessed through our senses. Empirical science doesn't help us with historical events because those events cannot be repeated. For instance, we can't use empirical science to prove the assassination of Abraham Lincoln. On the other hand, forensic science is used to study past, unrepeatable events. With forensic science, one must look at evidence and use logic to draw conclusions. Forensic science is used in archaeology, criminal investigations, cryptology (the study of codes), and even SETI (Search for Extraterrestrial Intelligence).

In proving the existence of a historical figure, it all comes down to documentation – historical records. Alexander the Great and Caesar Augustus lived before the invention of the printing press and the modern technology and information age. Ancient manuscripts were written on papyrus, made from plant reeds, which lasted only about 10 years before falling apart. Later, ancient manuscripts were written on parchment or vellum, both made from animal skins, which could last much longer than papyrus but were still fragile.

Additionally, a shortage of ancient manuscripts can be partially blamed on the many conflicts and wars of ancient times. Fire was a common weapon for ancient armies. For example, the ancient library of Alexandria, Egypt was renowned for its collection of manuscripts but much of the library was destroyed during several conflicts. Because of the lack of modern means of copying and saving information, sadly many ancient manuscripts have been lost to us forever.

When we turn to the New Testament, the ancient records about Jesus, we find the individual "books" that compose the New Testament have survived remarkably well compared to other ancient manuscripts.

THE SOURCES

To start, let's compare the sources for our information about Jesus to sources for two other famous ancient people: Alexander the Great and Caesar Augustus. Interestingly, no one raises questions about whether Alexander the Great or Caesar Augustus existed like they do about Jesus, but, as we'll see, the sources for our information about Jesus compare extremely well against the sources for these two other famous men from ancient times.

Furthermore, Alexander the Great and Caesar Augustus were rulers and conquerors of great empires — the most powerful, famous men of their time period — the exact type of people ancient historians wrote about. The fact that we know anything today about a poor rabbi from Nazareth is incredible.

ALEXANDER THE GREAT

We have two sources for our information about Alexander the Great. Both of these sources were written about 400 years after Alexander the Great lived.

CAESAR AUGUSTUS

We have five sources that give us the information we know about Caesar Augustus. One is a funeral writing, written at his death. One was written 50-100 years after his death. The last three were written 100-200 years after his death.

JESUS OF NAZARETH

For Jesus, we have four sources — the four Gospels found in the New Testament, each individually investigated, each containing both complementary and unique information. The four Gospels were written 25-60 years after Jesus' crucifixion, which means within the lifetime of those who knew Jesus and witnessed his ministry. (Jesus was crucified in about 30-33 AD, and all of the Gospels were written before 100 AD.) Two of the Gospels – Matthew and John – were written by two of Jesus' original twelve disciples, where the other two – Mark and Luke – were written by disciples of Jesus' apostles, Paul and Peter. This means the four sources we have for knowing about Jesus' life come from eyewitnesses.

Further, we also have Paul's letters, which are collected in the New Testament, which attest to Jesus' ministry, crucifixion, resurrection, and deity. The majority of Paul's letters, historians agree, were written before the four Gospels.

EARLY CREEDS

Historians also agree that Paul recorded several creeds of the early church that existed before he wrote them down in his letters. The earliest is found in **1 Corinthians 15:3-7**:

For I delivered to you as of first importance what I also received: that Christ died for our sins in accordance with the Scriptures, that he was buried, that he was raised on the third day in accordance with the

Scriptures, and that he appeared to Cephas,[18] then to the twelve. Then he appeared to more than five hundred brothers at one time, most of whom are still alive, though some have fallen asleep. Then he appeared to James, then to all the apostles.

This creed is widely accepted by scholars as being dated – at most! – two to five years after Jesus' crucifixion. Even atheist New Testament scholar Gerd Ludemann believes the creed was created before the appearance of the resurrected Jesus to Paul. Further, some scholars believe the creed appeared within months of Jesus' crucifixion.

Another early creed appears in Paul's letter to the Philippians:

Have this mind among yourselves, which is yours in Christ Jesus, who, though he was in the form of God, did not count equality with God a thing to be grasped, but emptied himself, by taking the form of a servant, being born in the likeness of men. And being found in human form, he humbled himself by becoming obedient to the point of death, even death on a cross. Therefore God has highly exalted him and bestowed on him the name that is above every name, so that at the name of Jesus every knee should bow, in heaven and on earth and under the earth, and every tongue confess that Jesus Christ is Lord, to the glory of God the Father. (Philippians 2:5-11)

THE MANUSCRIPTS

But what about actual physical manuscripts – I mean, manuscripts we can actually hold in our hands and read with our own eyes today. Since we already covered how perishable these ancient manuscripts were, it's logical to ask, *How many have survived until this day?*

---

[18] The apostle Peter.

Who Jesus Ain't

First, because of the fragileness of ancient manuscripts, as far as we know, *no* original ancient manuscripts have survived to this day. Meaning, we don't have the actual first manuscripts written in the hands of the New Testament authors – or any other originals from any other ancient writers for that matter. These ancient writings have survived through the tedious work of scribes, who copied them by hand to preserve these important works for future generations. We do have actual ancient manuscripts that have survived until today, but just not the *originals*.

So, how does the New Testament compare to other ancient manuscripts?

- For Aristotle, we have 49 ancient manuscripts.
- For Sophocles, we have 193 ancient manuscripts.
- For Plato's tetralogies, we have 7 ancient manuscripts.
- For Homer's *The Iliad*, we have 643 ancient manuscripts.
- For the New Testament, we have about 5,686 ancient manuscripts in the original Greek, either in part or in whole. Plus, there are about 9,000 other ancient manuscripts of the New Testament books in other languages.

The earliest ancient manuscript piece of the New Testament we have today is a fragment from the Gospel of John (18:31-33, 37-38).[19] This fragment was found in Egypt and has been dated about 125-130 AD, but could be as early as 90 AD. The dating puts it within 40 years of the original writing of the Gospel of John, and the fragment proves that the Gospel had spread as far as Egypt in that short period!

---

[19] John 18:31-33, 37-38: "Pilate said to them, 'Take him yourselves and judge him by your own law.' The Jews said to him, 'It is not lawful for us to put anyone to death.' This was to fulfill the word that Jesus had spoken to show by what kind of death he was going to die… So Pilate entered his headquarters again and called Jesus and said to him, 'Are you the King of the Jews?'"

New Testament scholar F.F. Bruce wrote, "There is better evidence for the New Testament than any other ancient book."[20]

TEXTUAL CRITICISM: IT AIN'T THE TELEPHONE GAME

Because of this wealth of manuscripts, scholars can easily compare the ancient New Testament manuscripts through a process called *textual criticism* and easily identify errors and variants made by the scribes. Expectantly, the scribes, who copied texts by hand, were not perfect, but most mistakes are nothing to be concerned about. The vast majority are spelling mistakes or other simple copying mistakes (like omitting or adding small words or reversing the order of words), which have no effect on how the New Testament is understood.

Often skeptics try to portray the passing on of the New Testament over time like the *Telephone Game* that you may have played in school as a child. In the Telephone Game, someone whispers a sentence into someone's ear, and then the second person whispers the sentence into another person's ear, and so on down the line. When the last person receives the sentence, he says it out loud for all to hear. In the vast majority of cases, the sentence is severely corrupted and changed by the time it reaches the end of the line. But this analogy is downright inaccurate. Anyone who claims this is how the New Testament was passed on to us today is basing that belief on assumption and not research, and they're illustrating their ignorance of textual criticism.

Instead of thinking of the passing on of the New Testament as a straight telephone line, think of it as a family tree with many branches giving birth to many more branches. A family tree spreads in many directions as it multiplies; it doesn't move in a straight line. Thus, if one branch

---

[20] *The New Testament Documents: Are They Reliable?* by F.F. Bruce (William B. Eerdmans Publishing Company and InterVarsity Press, 1981).

becomes corrupted, the many other branches will *not* be corrupted in the same way.

Further, the Telephone Game analogy utterly fails because the message is only whispered and it cannot be repeated. The New Testament, on the other hand, is a written document; it can be reread and rechecked.

To sum up, the Telephone Game has only one line of transmission; the message is only whispered; and repeating is not allowed. On the other hand, the New Testament was passed on through many lines of transmission; it was written; and, therefore, it can be reread, examined, and compared.

Hey, Here's a Helpful Illustration

Imagine we had five ancient manuscripts and we notice variations among all five of them in the same sentence. This sounds like a big problem, but see if you can pick which line is the original:

1. **Christ Jesus is the Savior of the world.**
2. **Jesus Christ is the Savior of the word.**
3. **Jesus is the Savior of the word.**
4. **Jesus Christ is the Savior of the world.**
5. **Jesus Christ is Savior of the world.**[21]

Highlighting the differences between each sentence will help us narrow the choices down:

1. **Christ Jesus** is the Savior of the **world**.
2. Jesus Christ is the Savior of the **word**.

---

[21] This illustration has been adapted and expanded from *The Ten Most Important Things You Can Say to a Mormon*, Chapter 3:"The Bible is God's Word and is Trustworthy" by Ron Rhodes (Harvest House Publishers, 2001).

3. Jesus [Missing: **Christ**] is the Savior of the **word**.
4. Jesus Christ is the Savior of the **world**.
5. Jesus Christ is [Missing: **the**] Savior of the **world**.

First, we can conclude that the original sentence started with "Jesus Christ," since only Sentence #1 starts with "Christ Jesus." Likewise, we can easily conclude Sentence #3 should include the word "Christ" and Sentence #5 should include the word "the" since all the others do.

Notice none of these variations so far affect the meaning of the sentence. Though we don't show this in this illustration, let me point out again, the vast majority of mistakes in the manuscripts by the scribes are simple spelling and grammar mistakes in the original language of the New Testament, ancient Koine ("common") Greek, which make no difference when the Greek is translated into English or any other language.

Finally, we have the variation of "world" versus "word." This is a tougher challenge to solve because this variation *does* affect the sentences' meanings and three of the sentences read "world" and two read "word." If it were the case that some of the manuscripts contained a nonsense word instead, like "Savior of the *worl*," the correct choice would be easy. In this case, I think most would agree "world" makes more sense than "word," and since more manuscripts have "world" than "word," it's the safer bet. But how can we be certain?

This is why we're fortunate to have many, many, many other manuscripts to compare than just these five! Specifically, we can look at those that were written before these manuscripts. The variation or mistake shouldn't have appeared yet in many of the earlier copies. In textual criticism, the rule of thumb is generally *the older the manuscript, the better*. In our illustration, it's likely the vast majority of the manuscripts will read "world." Thus, we can be confident that the original, correct sentence is **Sentence #4: *Jesus Christ is the Savior of the world*.**

This is how textual criticism works. Of course, this is simplified for the sake of illustration, but, as you can see, it's not all that hard spotting the original wording by comparing the manuscripts.

There was no central power controlling the copying of the New Testament. Churches were simply sharing the writings with other churches, and they would copy them and pass them on and on and on. One church may have the Gospel of Mark, and another church may have three of Paul's letters, so they would share and copy and pass on. Archaeological evidence proves the New Testament spread rapidly across the ancient world. Thus, in ancient terms, this means the New Testament *went viral*! And because of this, we have a wealth of ancient manuscripts that can be compared to and contrasted against each other.

Textual criticism has found only 1% of the variants have any effect on the meaning of the text, and *none* of these come close to affecting any Christian beliefs. Textual critics are positive the New Testament we read today is 99% accurate to the originals.

Further, the early church fathers, who lived between 90-160 AD, shortly after the completion of the New Testament, quoted the New Testament so extensively that the majority of the New Testament can be reconstructed from their sermons and writings alone. So, even if we had no ancient manuscripts of the New Testament, we'd still have much of it preserved in the writings of the early church fathers. Obviously, these early church fathers were quoting from manuscripts written earlier than their own writings.

SO, WHAT DOES THIS TELL US?

First, our current New Testament is faithful to the originals. Despite a lot of assumptions about the Bible being corrupted over time, the evidence says otherwise.

Who Jesus Ain't

Secondly, even secular historians consider the New Testament an excellent historical source, but the supernatural events the New Testament reports make them skeptical of its historical accuracy. Because of this, many non-Christian historians gladly use it to learn of Jesus and the time period but ignore the supernatural aspects of it. You see, their view of the New Testament has nothing to do with the evidence itself, but with their way of understanding the world, their *worldview*. If someone's worldview is that God doesn't exist, then of course he's not going to believe in the supernatural parts of the Bible. But if someone does believe in God, then believing in the miracles of the Bible isn't difficult at all.

Interestingly, scholars say that the time between the events of Jesus' life and the writing of the New Testament is much too short to allow legends and myths to develop, especially considering that people who witnessed Jesus were still living at the time of the writing of the New Testament. The writers present the New Testament as a historical record and provide names and other information so their contemporaries could investigate and confirm their claims about Jesus. Where one can argue that this alone doesn't prove the truth of the New Testament, it must be recognized that the New Testament doesn't have the unspecific, "other-world-ness" of mythology. (More about this below.)

Lastly, no evidence of an early record of a strictly "human-only" Jesus or any other alternative view of Jesus exists. If the New Testament originally had Jesus as only a normal man, but later made him supernatural, where is the evidence of these early versions of the New Testament? I've often heard skeptics say they don't believe in God because of a lack of evidence. Yet, when it comes to Jesus, many people (even some professing Christians) ignore the best evidence and base their ideas about who Jesus is on creations of their own mind.

There is also mention of Jesus outside of the Bible in ancient writings by non-Christians, but these were all written later than the New Testament. Even if someone doesn't believe in God or that Jesus is the Son of God or that the New Testament is the inspired Word of God, he or she – after evaluating the evidence – should still recognize that the New Testament is our best, most reliable source for learning about Jesus.

We'll spend some time in Chapter 7 looking at these ancient references to Jesus by non-Christians outside of the Bible, but for now we have answered our opening question:

How do we know about Jesus?

We know about Jesus from the reliable, well-preserved record of the New Testament.[22]

THE UNIQUENESS OF THE NEW TESTAMENT

Though this book is specifically about Jesus of Nazareth and not the New Testament itself, it makes sense to spend some more time looking at our primary source for learning about Jesus.

---

[22] Various sources contributed to or confirm the information in this chapter, including: *How We Got the Bible* by Neil R. Lightfoot (Baker Books, 2010); *The Case For the Real Jesus* by Lee Strobel (Zondervan, 2007); *The Case For Christ* by Lee Strobel (Zondervan, 1998); *I Don't Have Enough Faith To Be an Atheist* by Norman Geisler & Frank Turek (Crossway, 2004); *Holman QuickSource Guide to Christian Apologetics* by Doug Powell (Holman Reference, 2006); *Can We Still Believe the Bible?* by Craig Blomberg (Brazos Press, 2014); *The Heresy of Orthodoxy* by Andreas Kostenberger & Michael Kruger (Crossway, 2010); *Scripture Alone* by James White (Bethany House, 2004); and *Misquoting Truth: A Guide to the Fallacies of Bart Ehrman's "Misquoting Jesus"* by Timothy Paul Jones (IVP Books, 2007).

Who Jesus Ain't

Though I've done some research on Islam, Mormonism, Buddhism, and Jehovah's Witnesses, and I have a basic understanding of other major religions, I wouldn't want to portray these religions in shallow ways as so many do with my own faith, Christianity. Since I'm constantly reading attacks on Christianity by people with strong opinions but a poor understanding of Christianity, I wouldn't want to do the same.

That being said, let me point out some things I've found to be unique about Christianity and the New Testament. I'm not going to comment specifically about other faiths or their scriptures, but encourage you to research these things about the New Testament and compare and contrast them to other faiths.

1. Style

Many other religions' scriptures are simply sayings or teachings said or written by their founder, but the New Testament is unique in that it's made up of histories and letters. The letters in the New Testament are written primarily to young churches to address certain issues or questions about their faith. Of course, within these letters were given Christian theology and application.

These men were chosen by Jesus to be his apostles and inspired by the Holy Spirit to write the Word of God. Though they were certainly aware of the authority given to them by God and their writings were recognized by the first Christians as divinely inspired, these letters have a much different feel than if someone decided to sit down and simply draw up a religion's manifesto. The first Christians had experienced something incredible and were trying to live according to what they experienced. Just as Christians practice today, sometimes more mature Christians need to give guidance and advice to their brothers and sisters in Christ.

Furthermore, the narrative histories contain the words of Jesus, but they're also deeply concerned with reporting not just what he *said* but what he *did*. Jesus' miracles – called "signs" in John's Gospel and elsewhere in the Bible – are important because they confirm he's of God. Anyone can claim to be from God, but true miracles explicitly prove this. Frankly, Jesus' execution and resurrection were more important than anything he said. Likewise, the Book of Acts reports the apostles, empowered by Jesus and the Holy Spirit, also performed miracles to confirm the truth of their message. The writers of the New Testament understood, as the saying goes, actions speak louder than words.

2. History

Moreover, the historical narratives about Jesus and his apostles – the Gospels and Acts – are rooted in history. The New Testament doesn't have the fuzzy, "other-worldliness" of mythology. Mythology takes place in an unspecified time and location; it's floating out in Never-Never-Land somewhere. The New Testament is undeniably rooted in history.

Ancient historians Josephus (a non-Christian Jew, writing about 90-95 AD), Pliny (a Roman senator, writing about 111 AD), and Cornelius Tacitus (a Roman proconsul, writing in 115 AD) all confirm the existence of Jesus, his crucifixion, and the belief of his followers that Jesus had resurrected from the dead, and about seven other ancient non-Christian sources confirm information about Jesus and early Christians.[23]

Furthermore, 84 facts in the last 16 chapters of Acts alone have been confirmed by historical and archaeological research, and in the Gospel of Luke, 11 historically proven leaders appear in the first three chapters

---

[23] See more about this in Chapter 7.

alone.[24] New archaeological discoveries have continually supported the reliability of the biblical record, including the discovery of Jacob's Well, a building inscription of the name Pontius Pilate, and an ossuary containing the bones of Caiaphas, the high priest who helped orchestrate the crucifixion of Jesus.

Throughout the Gospels and Acts, supernatural events, such as miracles, are recorded in the same plain, unembellished language as the parts that record everyday details – the same straightforward language other ancient histories use. Thirty-five miracles appear side-by-side 84 proven facts in the book of Acts alone.[25]

This lack of embellishment isn't seen in later, false "gospels," written in the second century, long after Jesus' apostles were dead. These forged, false gospels include the *Gospel of Mary* and the *Gospel of Judas*. These were written about 100 years after the New Testament by a cult that combined Greek philosophy and Christianity called *Gnosticism*. In these Gnostic writings, we see the beginnings of myth introduced into the story of Jesus as they portray Jesus even more supernaturally than the true Gospels. For example, the *Gospel of Peter* reports the following about Jesus' resurrection:

"...again they saw three men come forth from the tomb, and two of them supporting one, and a cross following them. And the heads of the two reached to heaven, but the head of him who was led by them overpassed the heavens. And they heard a voice from the heavens, saying, 'You have preached to them that sleep.' And a response was heard from the cross, 'Yes.'"

---

[24] See Chapter 10:"Do We Have Eyewitness Testimony About Jesus?" in *I Don't Have Enough Faith To Be an Atheist* by Norman Geisler & Frank Turek.
[25] See Chapter 10:"Do We Have Eyewitness Testimony About Jesus?" in *I Don't Have Enough Faith To Be an Atheist* by Norman Geisler & Frank Turek.

Yes, you read that right: a walking, talking cross! Not to mention three guys with really big heads.

Moreover, all four Gospels and Acts show a firsthand understanding of 1st-Century Jewish culture, 1st-Century Judean events, and Judean geography, which are not found in later false gospels since they were written in a different time and place by non-Jews.

C.S. Lewis, Oxford professor, expert of ancient mythology, and former atheist, wrote, "As a literary historian, I am perfectly convinced that whatever else the Gospels are, they are not legends. I have read a great deal of legend, and I am quite clear that they are not the same sort of thing."[26]

3. Eyewitnesses

The Gospels, the histories of Jesus' ministry, and Acts, the history of the apostles and the early church, mention the names of specific people, rulers, and places. Not only were many of the writers of the New Testament eyewitnesses, but they constantly point the reader to other eyewitnesses to confirm what they are writing. All of the New Testament was written within the lifetime of those who lived during the events reported. The New Testament wasn't written generations after the events when no one was around to refute any inaccuracies, legend, or mythology added into them. The writers of the New Testament are essentially telling their readers, "Here are the facts – the people, the places. Go look into it yourself."

For example,

For I delivered to you as of first importance what I also received, that Christ died for our sins according to the Scriptures, and that He was

---

[26] *God in the Dock: Essays on Theology and Ethics* by C.S. Lewis.

buried, and that He was raised on the third day according to the Scriptures, and that He appeared to Cephas,[27] then to the twelve. After that He appeared to more than five hundred brethren at one time, most of whom remain until now, but some have fallen asleep; then He appeared to James, then to all the apostles; and last of all, as to one untimely born, He appeared to me[28] also. (1 Corinthian 15:3-8)

...Agrippa the king and Bernice arrived at Caesarea and greeted Festus... And as he was saying these things in his defense, Festus said with a loud voice, "Paul, you are out of your mind; your great learning is driving you out of your mind." But Paul said, "I am not out of my mind, most excellent Festus, but I am speaking true and rational words. For the king knows about these things, and to him I speak boldly. For I am persuaded that none of these things has escaped his notice, for this has not been done in a corner. (Acts 25:13, 26:24-26)

Moreover, note how Luke starts his Gospel and the amount of specific details he includes throughout:

Inasmuch as many have undertaken to compile an account of the things accomplished among us, just as they were handed down to us by those who from the beginning were eyewitnesses and servants of the word, it seemed fitting for me as well, having investigated everything carefully from the beginning, to write it out for you in consecutive order, most excellent Theophilus; so that you may know the exact truth about the things you have been taught. (Luke 1:1-4)

In the fifteenth year of the reign of Tiberius Caesar, Pontius Pilate being governor of Judea, and Herod being tetrarch of Galilee, and his brother Philip tetrarch of the region of Ituraea and Trachonitis, and Lysanias tetrarch of Abilene, during the high priesthood of Annas and Caiaphas, the word of God came to John the son of Zechariah in the

---

[27] The apostle Peter.
[28] The apostle Paul.

wilderness. And he went into all the region around the Jordan, proclaiming a baptism of repentance for the forgiveness of sins. (Luke 3:1-3)

Can you imagine how easily someone could refute the Gospel of Luke at the time it was written if it weren't accurate?

Christianity began in Jerusalem, as any historian will tell you. If the first Christians invented stories about Jesus in the exact location and exact time period of the events recorded in the New Testament, what would skeptics do? They would say, "Where are your witnesses?" and "I was here and didn't see any of that happen!" And, even more likely, they would've gotten Jesus' dead body out of the tomb and dragged it into the streets to prove he hadn't been raised. But this didn't happen. Christianity grew in Jerusalem and spread from it.

In 1993, the FBI killed in a gunfight David Koresh, leader of the Branch Davidians cult. If the cult members claimed Koresh had risen from the dead three days later, the FBI would've produced the body for all to see. On the other hand, if Koresh did, in fact, rise from the dead, I'm sure we'd all be living next door to some Branch Davidians today. Modern cults grow by isolating their members. Yet, the Christian church grew shortly after Jesus' crucifixion in Jerusalem, the exact location where the events occurred – and even within a hostile environment, where their beliefs were seen as blasphemy and even treason by the Romans and their fellow Jews.

4. "Publicness"

It's important to understand that Christianity is a "very public" religion. Anyone can walk into a worship service and join in, and anyone can walk into a bookstore and buy a Bible. There are no secrets. This is Christianity's "publicness" (Yes, I probably made up that word), and Christianity has always been a public faith.

What I mean by this is that Jesus preached in public for all to hear, and his miracles were performed in public for all to see, including his most important miracle: his death and resurrection. If God were to reveal his Word to the world, would he keep it a secret? If God were going to break into the world with a new revelation, would he only perform a miracle for one person to witness? This "publicness" is not the case with other religions. With many, the founder of the religion was the only one to experience any encounter with God or witness any miracle from God.

Before we move on to the final unique feature of Christianity and the New Testament, I want to encourage you again to look into all that I'm writing here and then do the same for other faiths.

5. Salvation is Not Earned

Lastly, Christianity is the only faith that teaches that salvation is through God's mercy alone. In all other faiths salvation must be earned.

Christianity is not a faith where favor with God is earned through "good works." We all have sin, and sin separates us eternally from a perfectly good, holy God. Christians believe God became a man called Jesus of Nazareth, lived the perfect life that we cannot, and willingly died, taking the punishment we deserve, so we can benefit through a repaired relationship with him.

We can't earn this; we don't deserve it; it's a free gift from God that we can only receive. Once we understand this gift and receive it, yes, it changes us, and we do "good works." But the works are the result of salvation, not the means of salvation. We love others out of obedience and love for the God who loved us first. No other religion that I have come across teaches this.

CHAPTER 4:
JESUS AIN'T
AN ONLY CHILD

Where's Joseph?

It appears that by the time Jesus started his ministry in his thirties, Joseph, his earthly father, had passed away. Where Jesus' siblings and his mother Mary appear in the Gospels during Jesus' ministry and Mary was even present at his crucifixion,[29] there is never any involvement by Joseph.

The only verse that may challenge this conclusion is in **John 6:42**: *"They were saying, 'Is not this Jesus, the son of Joseph, whose father and mother we know?'"* The present tense verb of "know" has led some to speculate that Joseph was still alive, but few find it convincing

---

[29] John 19:25-27.

enough to override the obvious lack of Joseph throughout Jesus' ministry, especially since there are sections in the Gospels and Acts where Mary and Jesus' siblings appear.

Then again, though we have four independent records about Jesus' life, they primarily focus on his ministry; only Matthew and Luke record anything about his early life, and what the Gospels record of his ministry are a small handful of episodes from three years of ministry. Is it possible Joseph was home, working hard in his trade at this time? Is it possible that none of the events the Gospel writers chose to record about Jesus' ministry involved his father? (After all, the appearances of Mary and Jesus' siblings are scattered and few.) Or is it possible Joseph was alive at the beginning of Jesus' ministry, but he died shortly after it started? Since the Gospels focus mostly on the years of Jesus' ministry, if his earthly father died during it, wouldn't there be some mention of it? But let's face it, any book about anyone's life is going to leave out much more than it can include, and Jesus is no exception.

But most scholars believe Joseph has passed away by the time of Jesus' ministry. How old was Jesus when Joseph died? We don't know. But Joseph lived long enough for Jesus to have several siblings.

Jesus, being the firstborn son, would have had a considerable amount of responsibility, especially if Joseph had passed away. We also know from the Gospels that Jesus' had four half-brothers ("half" because Jesus was biologically related to Mary but not Joseph since he was conceived through the Holy Spirit) and at least two sisters.[30] Just like the Gospels don't tell us how old Jesus was when Joseph died, we don't know the age differences between Jesus and his brothers and sisters.

---

[30] Mark 6:3.

Jesus' Brothers: What Changed?

Nothing in the New Testament indicates that Mary remained a virgin for all of her life. (Sorry, my Catholic friends.) The Greek word used doesn't indicate Jesus' brothers were cousins, as some argue, and there's absolutely no evidence for the view that Joseph had children from a previous marriage as others have suggested. Most of all, **Matthew 1:24-25** clearly states that Joseph and Mary had normal sexual relations after Jesus' birth:

"When Joseph woke from sleep, he did as the angel of the Lord commanded him: he took his wife, but knew her not until she had given birth to a son. And he called his name Jesus."

In the Hebrew language, the phrase "to know" your wife or husband meant knowing him or her intimately through sex. Joseph "knew her not until" after Jesus was born. Note this alternative, accurate translation:

"And Joseph awoke from his sleep and did as the angel of the Lord commanded him, and took Mary as his wife, but kept her a virgin until she gave birth to a Son; and he called His name Jesus."[31]

Furthermore, this idea of Mary's perpetual virginity implies that sex within marriage is sinful, which doesn't jive with Christian theology or ethics. God created sex for married couples to be fruitful and multiply, but he also created it for husbands and wives to enjoy together; there's nothing sinful or "dirty" about enjoying sex within marriage. (If you don't think this idea is in the Bible, then you haven't read the Song of Solomon in the Old Testament!) Mary is a wonderful example of a godly woman, but she had – like all of us – sin. Yet, she wasn't guilty of

---

[31] This translation is from the NASB. All other verses in this book are quoted from the ESV translation.

sexual sin – not because she remained a virgin, but because she had sex with her husband within the covenant of marriage as God intended.

Jesus had four half-brothers: James, Joseph (Joses), Judas (Jude), and Simon. **John 7:1-5** states they didn't "believe in" Jesus during his ministry, and here they even sarcastically mock Jesus, encouraging him to go to Judea where people were looking to kill him:

After this Jesus went about in Galilee. He would not go about in Judea, because the Jews were seeking to kill him. Now the Jews' Feast of Booths was at hand. So his brothers said to him, "Leave here and go to Judea, that your disciples also may see the works you are doing. For no one works in secret if he seeks to be known openly. If you do these things, show yourself to the world." For not even his brothers believed in him. (John 7:1-5)

Other passages indicate there was tension between Jesus and his family, including his mother, during his ministry:

And when Jesus had finished these parables, he went away from there, and coming to his hometown he taught them in their synagogue, so that they were astonished, and said, "Where did this man get this wisdom and these mighty works? Is not this the carpenter's son? Is not his mother called Mary? And are not his brothers James and Joseph and Simon and Judas? And are not all his sisters with us? Where then did this man get all these things?" And they took offense at him. But Jesus said to them, "A prophet is not without honor except in his hometown and in his own household." (Matthew 13:53-57)

Notice Jesus says that a prophet is not honored both in his hometown and "in his own household."

And his mother and his brothers came, and standing outside they sent to him and called him. And a crowd was sitting around him, and they said to him, "Your mother and your brothers are outside, seeking you." And he answered them, "Who are my mother and my brothers?" And looking about at those who sat around him, he said, "Here are my mother and my brothers! For whoever does the will of God, he is my brother and sister and mother." (Mark 3:31-35)

These details would be extremely embarrassing to include in a record about a first century rabbi's ministry, let alone a record claiming this man is the long-awaited Messiah. Because of this, even non-Christian and skeptical New Testament scholars accept these as authentic details from Jesus' life. If the New Testament writers were just making up stories about Jesus to make him look like the Messiah, this would do much more harm than good.

Amazingly, despite evidence of Jesus' brothers not following him or believing in him during his ministry, we actually find two letters by Jesus' brothers in the New Testament: James and Jude. After Jesus' resurrection and ascension, we even find Mary and Jesus' brothers (and probably sisters[32]) together with the disciples, joining them in prayer:

And when they had entered, they went up to the upper room, where they were staying, Peter and John and James and Andrew, Philip and Thomas, Bartholomew and Matthew, James the son of Alphaeus and Simon the Zealot and Judas the son of James. All these with one accord were devoting themselves to prayer, together with the women and Mary the mother of Jesus, and his brothers. (Acts 1:13-14)

We know next to nothing about Jesus' brother Jude (and his other siblings) but considerably more about his brother James from the New Testament and a few sources outside of the Bible. James is mentioned several times in the New Testament as a follower of Jesus Christ *after* Jesus' death and resurrection, including **Galatians 1:18-19**, where Paul

---

[32] We know Jesus had at least two sisters (Mark 6:3). The original Greek word here could mean either "brothers" or "brothers and sisters," sort of like how "man" in English can refer to a male or to all humans, male and female.

refers to him as an apostle of Jesus and "the Lord's brother." Not only did James have apostolic authority to write – inspired by the Holy Spirit – a letter that's included in the New Testament, but it's evident James held a prominent role in the first church in Jerusalem.[33]

James was known for devoutly following the Jewish Old Testament law as a Christian Jew,[34] yet when controversy in the early church arose about whether Gentile (non-Jewish) Christians should be circumcised according to Old Testament law, the church leaders gathered and James argued, along with Peter, that the Gentiles shouldn't have to be circumcised or bound to the Jewish religious and ritual laws. At this event (usually called the Jerusalem Council), James quotes **Amos 9:11-12** to show that God has always had in mind calling the non-Jews through grace to be among his people.

James held a place of authority in the first church in Jerusalem for about 20 years before being killed in 62 AD because of his faith in his older brother, Jesus of Nazareth. Ancient Jewish historian Josephus tells us in *Jewish Antiquities*,

"Convening the judges of the Sanhedrin, [Ananus] brought before them a man named James, the brother of Jesus, who was called Christ, and certain others. He accused them of having transgressed the law, and condemned them to be stoned to death."

So, what changed? What made James go from someone who thought his brother Jesus should be mocked to one of his brother's apostles, even helping to lead the first church in Jerusalem and dying because

---

[33] See Acts 12:17, 15:13-19, 21:18 and Galatians 2:9.
[34] See ancient Christian historian Eusebius' *Ecclesiastical History* 2.23, according to the ESV Study Bible.

of his faith in his half-brother? The answer is found in **1 Corinthians 15:3-7**, where Paul records the earliest church creed found in the New Testament:[35]

For I delivered to you as of first importance what I also received: that Christ died for our sins in accordance with the Scriptures, that he was buried, that he was raised on the third day in accordance with the Scriptures, and that he appeared to Cephas,[36] then to the twelve. Then he appeared to more than five hundred brothers at one time, most of whom are still alive, though some have fallen asleep. Then he appeared to James, then to all the apostles.

Yes, James had seen the risen Jesus. And once someone encounters the risen Christ, he is changed forever.

---

[35] See Chapter 3 in this book.
[36] The apostle Peter.

CHAPTER 5:
JESUS AIN'T
A PERFECT CHILD

The Mother of Jesus

James, Jude, and Jesus' other siblings didn't comprehend who he was until after his resurrection. As we'll see later in this book, his own disciples didn't get it at first either. But what people find most shocking is that Mary, his own mother, doesn't seem to completely understand who Jesus is also. As we saw in the last chapter, there was tension between Jesus and the rest of his family – and this includes his mother.[37] Again, this is extremely surprising to many, especially to someone with a highly revered view of Mary, like Roman Catholics. After all, if anyone knew for certain that Jesus was born from a virgin, it would be his mother! So, what are we to make of this?

---

[37] See Mark 3:31-35 again.

Who Jesus Ain't

When the angel Gabriel appears to Mary to tell her she'll be the mother of someone she's to name Jesus, the angel says,

He will be great and will be called the Son of the Most High. And the Lord God will give to him the throne of his father David, and he will reign over the house of Jacob forever, and of his kingdom there will be no end. (Luke 1:32-33)

When Mary asks how this will all happen since she is a virgin, Gabriel answers,

The Holy Spirit will come upon you, and the power of the Most High will overshadow you; therefore the child to be born will be called holy – the Son of God. (Luke 1:35)

So, Mary clearly knew her son was going to be special, yet the evidence in much of the rest of the Gospels seems to show that she didn't understand just how special. In fact, a first century Jew hearing the words of the angel would immediately understand him to be talking about the Messiah, the promised deliverer of the Jewish nation prophesied about in their Scripture (what we call the Old Testament). As Christians today, living post-resurrection and after the writing of the New Testament, we read all sorts of other significance into the angel Gabriel's words recorded in Luke 1. But to a first century Jew, the "Son of God" was the Messiah, who is a descendant of King David, who is human and not divine, and whose line will rule a political kingdom forever. Likely, the only unusual thing to Mary's ears would be the part about the virgin giving birth (but that prophecy is also found in the Old Testament[38]).

---

[38] Isaiah 7:14: "Therefore the Lord himself will give you a sign. Behold, the virgin shall conceive and bear a son, and shall call his name Immanuel [God with us]."

Based on the biblical evidence, it appears Mary lived with a tension between knowing her son was special and not understanding just how special he was. Think about it: even if an angel appeared to you and told you things about your child and your child was conceived in a miraculous way, would you just shrug whenever something else miraculous involving your child happened and say, "Yeah, I knew that would happen," or would you be continually amazed by every new miraculous event?

On the night of Jesus' birth, the shepherds arrive and tell of receiving word about Jesus from an angel,

And all who heard it wondered at what the shepherds told them. But Mary treasured up all these things, pondering them in her heart. (Luke 2:18-19)

When Simeon (more about him below) prophesies to Mary and Joseph about Jesus, we're told,

And his father and his mother marveled at what was said about him. (Luke 2:33)

When Mary and Joseph find the twelve-year-old Jesus in the Temple sitting among the teachers (more about this below also), we're told,

And when his parents saw him, they were astonished. (Luke 2:48)... And his mother treasured up all these things in her heart. (Luke 2:51)

Matthew doesn't state this outright, but you can imagine Mary's shock when foreigners from far, far away show up to see the child Jesus, not only bringing gifts, but even worshipping him:

And going into the house they saw the child with Mary his mother, and they fell down and worshiped him. Then, opening their treasures,

they offered him gifts, gold and frankincense and myrrh.
(Matthew 2:11)

Pregnant with Jesus' cousin, John the Baptist, Elizabeth exclaims to the pregnant Mary:

"Blessed are you among women, and blessed is the fruit of your womb! And why is this granted to me that the mother of my Lord should come to me? For behold, when the sound of your greeting came to my ears, the baby in my womb leaped for joy. And blessed is she who believed that there would be a fulfillment of what was spoken to her from the Lord." (Luke 1:42-45)

Though we're not told Mary expressed any surprise to Elizabeth's Spirit-led words, she composes a song humbly praising God for choosing her to be a part of his plan, and her wonder of the things that are happening is plain in it.[39] Mary is a wonderful, godly woman, and though she was "deeply troubled" at first by the words of the angel Gabriel, she also humbly said,

"Behold, I am the servant of the Lord; let it be to me according to your word." (Luke 1:38)

Mary marveled at her son, but she still didn't fully understand who he was. No one did – not until after the resurrection. Sometimes people point to when Jesus turned water into wine in **John 2** to argue against this view because it's Mary who comes to Jesus when the wine runs out at the wedding. They argue that Mary must have expected Jesus to do a miracle. Yet, reading the passage carefully doesn't support this idea; in fact, it's much more likely Mary came to him simply because he was

---

[39] Luke 1:46-55.

the eldest son of the family,[40] a position of great responsibility (especially since Joseph had likely passed away). She didn't expect him to do a miracle as if Jesus were some miracle-producing vending machine; she expected him to take the servants at the wedding and go find more wine!

The biblical evidence doesn't support the idea that Mary and Joseph's household lived with the adolescent Jesus performing works of wonder left and right like Gandalf the Wizard. I could be wrong, but I think Jesus was for the most part a regular, though unusual, kid – a sinless one! (We'll look at the only glimpse into Jesus' childhood in a moment.) As we'll discuss later in this book, Jesus' miracles served an important purpose in his ministry, and I think it's safe to say all of his miracles were performed after his ministry began. Yes, this is an argument from silence since we don't have extensive information about Jesus' youth, but even if Jesus performed some miracles before his ministry began, the evidence in the biblical record testifies that the majority were performed during his earthly ministry. Further, I don't think Jesus, God the Father, or the Holy Spirit would be so flippant about him performing miracles as it would get to the point where Mary would casually say to him, in effect, "Jesus, we need more wine. Go ahead and supernaturally manifest some out of thin air."

Perhaps the conflict between Jesus and his family began when he started neglecting his eldest-son responsibilities and his occupation as a carpenter[41] and began traveling throughout Judea proclaiming that the Kingdom of God has come.

Regardless of any family conflict, a mother always loves her son, and at the cross as Jesus hung dying, we find Mary there.

---

[40] Many scholars understand the situation this way, including D.A. Carson in his commentary *The Gospel of John* (Pillar New Testament Commentary).
[41] Mark 6:3.

... but standing by the cross of Jesus were his mother and his mother's sister, Mary the wife of Clopas, and Mary Magdalene. When Jesus saw his mother and the disciple whom he loved[42] standing nearby, he said to his mother, "Woman, behold, your son!" Then he said to the disciple, "Behold, your mother!" And from that hour the disciple took her to his own home. (John 19:25-27)

Other than Jesus, I doubt anyone suffered as much on that day as Mary as she witnessed the slow execution of her oldest son. Undoubtedly, the prophecy Simeon spoke directly to Mary when the infant Jesus was presented at the Temple rung in her ears:

"Behold, this child is appointed for the fall and rising of many in Israel, and for a sign that is opposed (and a sword will pierce through your own soul also), so that thoughts from many hearts may be revealed." (Luke 2:34-35)

But, it's also probable; all those wonders Mary witnessed, pondered, and "treasured up" in her heart suddenly made sense when she saw her dead son alive.

The Adolescence of Jesus

As we continue to explore what we can know about Jesus' life before his ministry, let's look at the two least-popular events of Jesus' life recorded in the Gospels.

Okay, I'll admit, saying these are the two most unpopular events of Jesus' life is an inflated claim, and a claim I can't back up. But bare with me: I only claim this because they fall outside the umbrella of the Christmas story (which is well-known not just with devout Christians

---

[42] Likely the disciple John, the writer of this Gospel.

but all of western society) and they fall outside the umbrella of Jesus' ministry (which is the primary focus of all four Gospels).

The two episodes I'm talking about are
(1) Jesus being presented in the Temple as an infant and
(2) Jesus in the Temple at 12-years-old.

Since neither of these events are essential to the Christmas story nor Jesus' ministry, it's no surprise Luke is the only Gospel writer to report them. Regardless, both events are fascinating and give us a glimpse into Jesus' family and youth.

The first episode takes place when Mary and Joseph present Jesus, as their firstborn, at the Temple and offer a sacrifice according to the Law of Moses.[43] (In Chapter 1, we looked at why their sacrifice of two doves and two pigeons illustrates to us their poverty.) The Holy Spirit had revealed to a devout, righteous man named Simeon that he wouldn't die before seeing the Messiah. Led by the Holy Spirit, Simeon immediately recognizes the child Jesus as God's *"salvation"* and *"a light for revelation to the Gentiles, and for glory to your people Israel."*[44] He praises God and blesses Joseph and Mary. Similarly, a widowed prophetess named Anna in the Temple *"at that very hour"* began thanking God and telling all who were waiting for the Messiah about Jesus.[45]

The second episode is recorded in Luke 2 immediately after the account about Simeon and Anna, but first we're told,

"And the child grew and became strong, filled with wisdom. And the favor of God was upon him." (Luke 2:40)

---

[43] Exodus 13:2.
[44] Luke 2:29-32.
[45] Luke 2:36-38.

Who Jesus Ain't

In the second episode, Jesus is twelve-years-old. This is the only story we have from Jesus' youth, when he's neither an infant (or perhaps a toddler) nor a grown man. This is also the last time we find any mention of Joseph in the Gospels, which leads most to assume he had passed away before the start of Jesus' ministry.

Jesus' family had traveled to Jerusalem for the Passover. This would've been done in a large caravan with others, most likely with their extended family. (There's no mention of Jesus' siblings here, but it could be because they weren't important to the story.)

When returning home to Galilee, it takes a day's journey before Mary and Joseph realize Jesus is not with the caravan! This may give us a good idea about the size of the caravan. Perhaps Mary and Joseph assumed Jesus' was safe with relatives. I've always visualized them assuming he was off playing with his cousins, probably because I was close to my own cousins growing up and always looked forward to our families getting together, and there were definitely times the adults lost track of us. Or maybe they assumed Jesus was off playing with some of his brothers and sisters, and when they located his siblings, we can imagine the conversation:

"James, Jude – where's Jesus?"

"Dad, we thought he was with you!"

However it happened, Luke tells us Joseph and Mary returned to Jerusalem and looked for Jesus for three days. Three days! Can you imagine how worried they were? But, finally, they find Jesus in the Temple *"sitting among the teachers, listening to them and asking them questions. And all who heard him were amazed at his understanding and his answers."*[46]

---

[46] Luke 2:46-47.

About 700 years earlier, a prophecy of the future Messiah tells us:

And the Spirit of the Lord shall rest upon him,
  the Spirit of wisdom and understanding,
  the Spirit of counsel and might,
  the Spirit of knowledge and the fear of the Lord. (Isaiah 11:2)

Luke ends this episode similarly to how he ends the other:

"And Jesus increased in wisdom and in stature and in favor with God and man." (Luke 2:52)

Jesus: Disobedient Child?

In this episode from Jesus' preteen days, we see that Jesus was very much an ordinary boy in many ways. He grew in stature and wisdom, like all boys. He even was a boy who got into trouble with his parents, even getting reprimanded by his mother:

And his mother said to him, "Son, why have you treated us so? Behold, your father and I have been searching for you in great distress." (Luke 2:48)

We can infer this wasn't an *intentional* disobedience of his parents since the New Testament teaches Jesus was without sin. Immediately afterwards, Luke – very intentionally, I believe – is sure to tell us Jesus returned to Nazareth and was obedient to them.[47] Luke didn't want his readers mistakenly believing the sinless Son of God broke one of the Ten Commandments – to honor his parents![48] We all know of children (and have been children ourselves!) who have gotten into big trouble

---

[47] Luke 2:51.
[48] Exodus 20:12.

with their parents not because of open, willful defiance, but because of innocent impulsiveness and curiosity.

These episodes are interesting and beautiful because, like the other aspects of Jesus' family and early life, it shows the humanness of Jesus Christ mingled with the wonders of his divine identity. Later, we'll look at Jesus' godliness, but Jesus was human also. Christians believe Jesus to be completely man and completely God – two natures in one person.[49] How these two natures commingle in one person is hard to wrap our heads around, but this episode shows us that Jesus, though God in the flesh, grew not just physically, but mentally.

Also, just as Jesus grew in "wisdom and in stature and in favor with God and man," we're also told in the New Testament he *"learned obedience through what he suffered"*[50] making him both *"the founder and perfecter of our faith."*[51] Again, I don't think the writers of the New Testament mean to imply that Jesus was sinfully disobedient to God the Father, but that his suffering *perfected* his obedience of God. Before his life in the flesh, God the Son could claim perfection, but after facing trials and tribulations, his obedience is proven and even more complete. And by living such a sinless life and by dying on a cross, he founded the Christian faith. So, God the Son was perfect, but his life on the earth made him *more* perfect. In other words, on the earth, his perfectness was put to the test and proven in a way that it couldn't be when God the Son was wholly spirit - and Jesus passed the test beyond any doubt. Jesus was a sinless child as God in the flesh, but he also was a typical child that grew and matured.

We see self-awareness of his unique identity when Mary and Joseph find him in the Temple after three days. Mary scolds him, and Jesus replies, *"Why were you looking for me? Did you not know that I must*

---

[49] More on this in Chapter 8 of this book.

[50] Hebrews 5:8.

[51] Hebrews 12:2.

be in my Father's house?"[52] By referring to the Temple as "my Father's house," Jesus is showing an understanding of his one-of-a-kind relationship with God the Father. Unlike Christians today, Jews in Jesus' time didn't refer to God as "Father." In fact, to make such a statement would've been shocking, perhaps even blasphemous. The Old Testament does refer to God as the Father of Israel, and the father metaphor for God is used at times elsewhere in the Old Testament, but it's irregular. "Father" is the primary way Jesus refers to God; his frequency (and the intimacy) of referring to God in such a way would surely have caught the attention of his first century audience. In fact, the Jews of Jesus' time understood correctly that by doing so he was making himself equal with God, an understanding lost on many of us today and those not from the Jewish faith.

This is clearly seen in John 5, where Jesus calls himself the Son of God many times, and then we're told:

This was why the Jews were seeking all the more to kill him, because not only was he breaking the Sabbath, but he was even calling God his own Father, making himself equal with God. (John 5:18)

Furthermore, Jesus says,

"Whoever does not honor the Son does not honor the Father who sent him." (John 5:23)

Proclaiming oneself to be equal with God was a blasphemy worthy of public stoning to death in first century Judea. But the New Testament claims Jesus was telling the truth. Jesus is the unique Son of God, and only through our relationship with him do we get adopted into the family and are given the privilege of calling God our heavenly Father.[53]

---

[52] Luke 2:49.
[53] Romans 8:14-17; Galatians 4:3-7; Ephesians 1:4-5.

CHAPTER 6:
JESUS AIN'T
A MARCIONITE

Of all the chapter titles in this book, I'm fairly certain this chapter's title is the one that will have the most people puzzled, because most people probably will read the title and think, *What the heck is a Marcionite?* A Marcionite isn't a race of aliens from a distant galaxy or man-eating ogres from Middle Earth, but someone who shares the views of a man named Marcion.

Who's Marcion? Not long after the New Testament was completed by Jesus' first apostles, a man named Marcion of Sinope, a wealthy, influential person in the early church, became quite a controversial figure. You see, he believed there were two Gods in the Scriptures – an evil God of the Old Testament and a good God of the New Testament. Further, he went on to attempt to rid anything he perceived as Jewish from the Scriptures. This included getting rid of the whole Old Testament and purging the New Testament of anything he perceived as too Jewish. Thus, he made his own "bible" of only severely edited versions of Paul's letters and the Gospel of Luke. As you can probably guess, the early Christian church didn't like this all that much and proclaimed Marcion a heretic in about 144 AD. So, like many false teachers, Marcion moved on to cult-leader status and started his own church.[54]

Today, I doubt too many of us know of any Marcionites, but I certainly know of many people who like Jesus but not the "God of the Old Testament." In fact, I've heard that phrase "God of the Old Testament" used so many times, it almost seems Bible-believing Christians have subconsciously become polytheists, separating the God of the Bible into two "gods" like Marcion did. To be perfectly honest, there have been times when I've been wrestling with tough parts of the Old Testament and I've found myself wishing that I could just ignore the Old Testament and stay in the New.

But it's essential we understand that when Jesus walked the earth, all there was of the Bible is what Christians today call "the Old Testament," the Jewish Scripture. Our modern Protestant Bibles are made of 66 "books" – 39 works of literature in the Old Testament and 27 works of the New Testament. Protestant Christians and Jews agree on the 39 books of the Old Testament as God's Word. The Jews organize the books differently, having 24 books of Scripture instead of 39 books. For example, 1 and 2 Kings are just one book (called Kings) and 1 and 2 Chronicles are just one book (called – big surprise! – Chronicles), and the 12 Minor Prophets (Hosea, Joel, Amos, etc.) are considered one book. Roman Catholics have extra books in their Old Testament – ancient Greek texts (written during the time between the Old and New

---

[54] Just to be clear: Jesus was a Jew, as were his original twelve disciples and the vast majority of the first Christians. Therefore, any and all bigotry by anyone claiming to be Christian towards Jews is absolute logical absurdity – and sin.

Testaments) called *the Apocrypha*, which aren't recognized as Scripture by either Protestant Christians or Jews. (A little research shows why these additional books shouldn't be considered divine Scripture, but we won't get into it here.)

Jesus' first followers wrote the New Testament after Jesus' earthly ministry, resurrection, and ascension. Thus, when Jesus makes any reference to God's Word in the Gospels, he's talking solely about the Old Testament because that's all that existed at that time. The last book of the Old Testament was written around 435 BC – that is, 435 years before Jesus of Nazareth walked the earth. Ancient Jewish historian Josephus (37-100 AD) confirms this, writing,

"From Artaxerxes to our times a complete history has been written, but has not been deemed worthy of equal credit with the earlier records, because of the failure of the exact succession of the prophets."[55]

Did you follow that? No Jewish history that had been written since the time of Artaxerxes – about 464-423 BC – has been accepted as equal in authority to the Old Testament ("the earlier records") because the line of God's prophets had ceased ("the failure of the exact succession of the prophets"). In other words, Josephus is saying that there has been no new Scripture because there have been no new prophets. This is why John the Baptist drew so much attention when he started proclaiming the repentance of sins in the wilderness and preparing the way for Jesus. The Jews recognized that he was a prophet.[56] It had been over 400 years since the Jewish people had seen a prophet!

---

[55] from *Against Apion* 1.41.
[56] See Matthew 3:1-17 & John 1:19-34.

So, what does Jesus of Nazareth think of the Old Testament?

Between Jesus and his apostles, they quote the Old Testament 92 times to argue their positions.[57] Robert Plummer in *40 Questions About Interpreting the Bible* writes, "While Jesus frequently criticized distorted understandings of the [Old Testament], he never questioned the veracity [the accuracy, the truthfulness] of the Scriptures themselves."[58]

As you read through the New Testament, it becomes plain that Jesus and his apostles viewed the Old Testament as important, and this tells us that we can't fully understand the New Testament (and, thus, Jesus of Nazareth) without understanding the Old Testament.

As the Jews commonly did in the first century, Jesus often refers to the Jewish Scripture as "the Law" and "the Prophets" and also "the Psalms." Notice what he says about his relationship to the Old Testament:

"Do not think that I have come to abolish the Law or the Prophets; I have not come to abolish them but to fulfill them." (Matthew 5:17)

This is why Christians don't follow Old Testament Jewish rituals and religious practices; Jesus fulfilled them by his death on the cross. Jewish laws of religious behavior and ritual are no longer   necessary.[59] But Jesus didn't discard the Old Testament as if it had no value. In fact, immediately after, he says,

---

[57] See Chapter 14:"What Did Jesus Teach About the Bible?" in *I Don't Have Enough Faith To Be an Atheist* by Norman Geisler & Frank Turek.

[58] *40 Questions About Interpreting the Bible* by Robert Plummer (Kregel Publications, 2010).

[59] Important note: Christians still follow the Old Testament moral laws because they're based on God's design for creation and God's own unchanging holiness and goodness. Furthermore, many of these moral laws are reconfirmed in the New Testament.

Who Jesus Ain't

"For truly, I say to you, until heaven and earth pass away, not an iota, not a dot, will pass from the Law until all is accomplished. (Matthew 5:18)

Jesus is not doing away with even a tiny dot or pen stroke of the Old Testament until "all is accomplished." Some of this "all" was accomplished by his death on the cross, and the rest will find fulfillment at his Second Coming.

In **John 10**, as Jesus is about to be stoned to death for saying *"I and the Father are one,"*[60] he quotes **Psalm 82:1-8** from the Old Testament to refute his opponents, asking, *"Is it not written in your Law...?"*[61] By doing this, Jesus not only shows his conviction that the Scripture has authority over anything contrary to Scripture his opponents may say, but he also says, *"Scripture cannot be broken."*[62] Here, Jesus is affirming the authority of the Old Testament. Essentially he's saying, *I'm backing up my argument with Scripture, and since Scripture is from God, you can't argue against it – it's unbreakable.* Jesus is demonstrating his absolute confidence in the complete authority, reliability, and preservation of God's Word.

The most interesting thing to note here is that Jesus' whole argument from Psalm 82 relies on *only one word*. His opponents say they're going to stone him because he made himself equal with God. Jesus points out that judges are referred to as "gods" in Psalm 82:1-8. His point is that if judges, who in the context of ancient Israel were representatives of God, can be called "gods" (not in a literal sense), the title is even more appropriate for him, the Son of God.[63] His whole argument relies on that one word: "gods." Jesus is so confident that *every single word* in

---

[60] John 10:30.
[61] John 10:34.
[62] John 10:35.
[63] ESV Study Bible.

Scripture is divinely inspired and accurately preserved that he can base his whole argument on a single word!

This is the pattern seen throughout the Gospels; Jesus constantly points back to the Old Testament to refute his enemies. So much so, that when Satan tries to tempt Jesus away from his ministry[64] (and, thus, tempt him away from his redeeming death on the cross), what does Jesus do? Does Jesus call down a legion of angels? Does Jesus use his divine powers to put Satan in a Darth Vader choke hold? Does he engage Satan in an epic rap battle? No, he simply quotes the Old Testament. Three times Satan attempts to draw Jesus away from his mission and all three times Jesus simply quotes from the Old Testament book of Deuteronomy to defeat him.

It's important to notice that it's not just Jesus who uses Scripture during his attempted temptation. Satan himself uses Scripture, quoting from Psalm 91, to try to manipulate Jesus.[65] Instead of allowing God's Word to transform him, Satan misuses God's Word for his own selfish, evil desires. As the serpent, this is what Satan did in the Garden of Eden when he led Eve into disobeying God, plunging the creation into sin and rebellion. Satan distorts and questions God's words causing Eve to doubt them. Satan starts by asking, **"Did God actually say, 'You shall not eat of any tree in the garden'?"**[66] Not only does Satan lead Eve into questioning God's plain words, but he misrepresents them to manipulate Eve; God never said she couldn't eat of "any tree," only one.

Does this situation sound familiar? I'm sure it does. I'm sure you can think of plenty of examples of people (both Christians and non-Christians) manipulating God's Word in hopes of selfishly manipulating others for some personal gain. Instead of allowing God's Word to speak truth into their lives, instead of working to understand

---

[64] See Matthew 4:1-11; Luke 4:1-13.
[65] Matthew 4:6.
[66] Genesis 3:1.

the Scriptures correctly, too many people have ideas in their heads, and then they go looking for confirmation of those ideas in God's Word; and if they don't find confirmation there, instead of bowing to God's infinite wisdom, they manipulate the words of Scripture and misrepresent God's clear instruction. Never forget, this is exactly what Satan did.

This is one of the reasons Christians must know God's Word well – to identify and refute those who abuse Scripture. Christians must diligently read Scripture and work to understand it as the apostles intended it to be understood. Studying the Bible is a lifelong endeavor. There are many parts of the Bible a Christian will have to wrestle with before he or she grasps them – maybe for a long time. A strong understanding of the Bible certainly won't come from only listening to one sermon once a week.

During another confrontation, this time with the Sadducees, they challenge Jesus on the belief of the future resurrection of the dead.[67] The Sadducees didn't believe in the future resurrection. Jesus straight-up tells them,

"You are wrong, because you know neither the Scriptures nor the power of God." (Matthew 22:29)

Boom. Whoever said Jesus sugarcoats things? Clearly, he takes off the safety gear when it comes to sparring over the Old Testament Scripture. But, again, what's really interesting here is *how* Jesus uses the Scripture. Addressing the Sadducees' denial of the resurrection of the dead, Jesus, quoting **Exodus 3:6**, says,

...have you not read what was said to you by God: 'I am the God of Abraham, and the God of Isaac, and the God of Jacob'? He is not God of the dead, but of the living." (Matthew 22:31-32)

---

[67] Matthew 22:23-33.

Who Jesus Ain't

Where the example we looked at shortly before this relied wholly on *one word* ("gods"), Jesus' argument here relies wholly on *one point of grammar*: whether the sentence is *present tense* or *past tense*. Jesus points out that God said "I am" the God of Abraham, Isaac, and Jacob. In Exodus 3:6, God said this to Moses after Abraham, Isaac, and Jacob had been dead for centuries. But God said, "I am" their God, not "I was" their God. Since God used the present tense ("am"), not the past tense ("was"), he's *still* the God of Abraham, Isaac, and Jacob though we, on the earth, consider them dead. God's people never truly die!

In Scripture, believers who have passed away are said to be "asleep"[68] physically and in God's presence spiritually,[69] and at the Final Judgment God will reunite their spirits and bodies, resurrecting them, bringing them back to their natural state, as God created humankind as both body and spirit before sin and death entered the world. The God of the Bible isn't the God of death, but the God of life – and of the living! Jesus' whole argument against the Sadducees rests on the tense of the main verb in the sentence and nothing else.

Not only all that, but Jesus confirms all of the following from Old Testament:

- God created everything, a clear reference to Genesis 1-2 (Mark 13:19);
- God made humans male and female from the beginning, a clear reference to Adam and Eve (Matthew 19:4-5; Genesis 1-2);

---

[68] For example, see 1 Thessalonians 4:14; Acts 13:36.

[69] Philippians 1:21-25: "For to me to live is Christ, and to die is gain. If I am to live in the flesh, that means fruitful labor for me. Yet which I shall choose I cannot tell. I am hard pressed between the two. My desire is to depart and be with Christ, for that is far better. But to remain in the flesh is more necessary on your account. Convinced of this, I know that I will remain and continue with you all, for your progress and joy in the faith…"

- Noah, the flood, and the ark (Matthew 24:37-39; Luke 17:27; Genesis 6-9);
- Sodom and Gomorrah's destruction by fire and sulfur raining down from the sky (Matthew 10:15; Luke 10:12; Luke 17:28-29; Genesis 18-19);
- Jonah swallowed by the great fish (Matthew 12:40; Jonah 1-2);
- Moses and the burning bush (Luke 20:37; Exodus 3);
- Moses and his lifting of the bronze serpent on a pole in the wilderness (John 3:14; Numbers 21:4-9);
- Abraham as the forefather of the Jewish people, as well as the other patriarchs, Isaac and Jacob (John 8:56-58; Luke 20:37; Genesis 12-36);
- The prophet Elijah and the drought he predicted, as well as Elijah's protégé, the prophet Elisha (Luke 4:25-27; 1 Kings 17-18; 2 Kings 7);
- The prophets Daniel and Isaiah and their accurate prophecies (Matthew 24:15; Matthew 13:14-15);
- The murder of Abel, the son of Adam and Eve, by his brother Cain, and the murder of Zechariah. (Matthew 23:35; Genesis 4; 2 Chronicles 24:20-22)[70]

What's interesting about this last one is that Jesus refers to both the murder of Abel and Zechariah in the same statement as he rips into some religious hypocrites:

"Woe to you, scribes and Pharisees, hypocrites! For you build the tombs of the prophets and decorate the monuments of the righteous, saying, 'If we had lived in the days of our fathers, we would not have taken part with them in shedding the blood of the prophets.' Thus you witness against yourselves that you are sons of those who murdered the

---

[70] Much of this list was adapted from Chapter 14:"What Did Jesus Teach About the Bible?" in *I Don't Have Enough Faith To Be an Atheist* by Norman Geisler & Frank Turek.

prophets. Fill up, then, the measure of your fathers. You serpents, you brood of vipers, how are you to escape being sentenced to hell? Therefore I send you prophets and wise men and scribes, some of whom you will kill and crucify, and some you will flog in your synagogues and persecute from town to town, so that on you may come all the righteous blood shed on earth, from the blood of righteous Abel to the blood of Zechariah the son of Barachiah, whom you murdered between the sanctuary and the altar. Truly, I say to you, all these things will come upon this generation. (Matthew 23:29-36)

As Jesus is telling these unscrupulous religious leaders that they're the type who kill God's true prophets and teachers and they'll be held accountable for all of these murders, he mentions the murders of Abel, which occurs in Genesis, and Zechariah, which happens in 2 Chronicles. When it comes to the Old Testament Scripture, though Jews and Protestant Christians agree on the same exact works as God's Word, the Jews count and organize them differently than the Protestant Bible. As I mentioned above, Jews have 24 books, and Protestants have 39 books. The Protestant Old Testament starts with Genesis and ends with Malachi, but the Jewish Bible starts with Genesis and ends with Chronicles. So, by referring to Abel (Genesis) to Zechariah (Chronicles), Jesus is covering all of Jewish Scripture, from the first book to the last!

Preserved in the New Testament, Jesus' apostle Paul wrote the following in a letter to a young church leader named Timothy:

All Scripture is breathed out by God and profitable for teaching, for reproof, for correction, and for training in righteousness, that the man of God may be complete, equipped for every good work. (2 Timothy 3:16-17)

When we look at the many, many times Jesus refers back to the Old Testament, we see clearly that this is exactly how he uses Scripture: he uses it for debating and rebuking God's enemies and for training and teaching God's people. If this is how Jesus uses it, this is how Christians should use it – with the same conviction as Jesus – because the Old Testament is God-breathed and God-created.

The Old Testament - Can We Trust It?

In the book *According to Plan: The Unfolding Revelation of God in the Bible,* Graeme Goldsworthy writes, "The New Testament interpretation of the person and work of Jesus of Nazareth makes no sense if there is no substance to the historical claims of the Old Testament."[71]

So, we've clearly seen that Jesus had complete confidence in the Jewish Scripture as it existed in his day. But that was over 2,000 years ago; what if the Old Testament has been corrupted or changed since then? Textual criticism and other means help us to understand that the Jewish Scriptures were carefully preserved. But arguably one of the most important archaeological discoveries ever gives us complete confidence in the Old Testament: The Dead Sea Scrolls.

The Dead Sea Scrolls are a collection of both biblical and non-biblical Jewish writings discovered in large jars in caves near the Dead Sea, about 13 miles east of Jerusalem. The first writings were found in 1947, and more continued to be found until 1956. Most likely, a Jewish monk-like sect called the Essenes, who lived in the desert because they believed mainstream Judaism in Jerusalem had become corrupt, hid the writings in the caves to preserve them during the Jewish revolt against the Romans in 66-70 AD. It seems the Essenes understood what was coming – more Romans! – and Jerusalem and its great Temple were utterly destroyed by Roman armies in 70 AD.

---

[71] *According to Plan: The Unfolding Revelation of God in the Bible* by Graeme Goldsworthy (InterVarsity Press, 1991), Chapter 5:"We Know Him Through Scripture."

What's most important to our purposes here is that the Dead Sea Scrolls were about 1,000 years older than the surviving Old Testament hand-written manuscripts we had at that time – yes, 1,000 years older! Dated to before 66-70 AD, these Jewish documents, which included sections of all of the books of the Old Testament except Esther, existed at the time of Jesus and his followers! Thus, they proved beyond a shadow of a doubt that the Old Testament was carefully passed down to us and preserved. Comparing these ancient manuscripts to the manuscripts that were copied 1,000 years later showed that the Jewish scribes did an incredible job of preserving the original words through the centuries. Therefore, the Old Testament we read today is the same Old Testament Jesus read.

For example, 19 copies of sections of Isaiah, the Old Testament book with the most prophecies about the Messiah, were found with the Dead Sea Scrolls. Not only that, but a complete twenty-four-foot scroll of Isaiah was discovered with them, which includes all 66 chapters. It's dated at 100 BC, and it's the oldest known biblical scroll in existence. When compared to the next oldest complete Isaiah manuscript – dated 1,000 years later – we find they're 95% identical! The 5% of variations are mostly spelling differences or simple penmanship mistakes that affect no doctrine or belief.[72]

Jesus in the Old Testament?

Among all of these allusions to the Old Testament by Jesus in the Gospels, we find Jesus applying the Old Testament to himself, including Isaiah:

And he came to Nazareth, where he had been brought up. And as was his custom, he went to the synagogue on the Sabbath day, and he stood

---

[72] See Chapter 13:"Who Is Jesus: God? Or Just a Great Moral Teacher?" in *I Don't Have Enough Faith To Be an Atheist* by Norman Geisler & Frank Turek.

up to read. And the scroll of the prophet Isaiah was given to him. He unrolled the scroll and found the place where it was written,

"The Spirit of the Lord is upon me,
  because he has anointed me
  to proclaim good news to the poor.
He has sent me to proclaim liberty to the captives
  and recovering of sight to the blind,
  to set at liberty those who are oppressed,
to proclaim the year of the Lord's favor."

And he rolled up the scroll and gave it back to the attendant and sat down. And the eyes of all in the synagogue were fixed on him. And he began to say to them, "Today this Scripture has been fulfilled in your hearing." (Luke 4:16-21)

Jesus reads from **Isaiah 61:1-2**[73] and says it's about him, that he's the fulfillment of this prophecy written 700 years before his birth. In his ministry, Jesus proclaims the good news of freedom from sin and condemnation, and to confirm his divine authority, he gives sight to the blind. Interestingly, Jesus stops reading at 61:2, where the very next line reads, *"...and the day of vengeance of our God."* During Jesus' First Coming, he came to proclaim the good news of salvation. But Jesus will bring judgment with him at his return, his Second Coming.[74]

According to Jesus, not only are the prophecies in Isaiah about him, but all of the Old Testament is about him. Jesus says to a group of fellow Jews looking to kill him,

You search the Scriptures because you think that in them you have eternal life; and it is they that bear witness about me, yet you refuse to

---

[73] Though he adapts it by leaving some lines out and adding some, including a line from Isaiah 58:6.

[74] See Chapter 13 of this book.

come to me that you may have life… For if you believed Moses, you would believe me; for he wrote of me. But if you do not believe his writings, how will you believe my words?" (John 5:39-40, 46-47)

After his death and resurrection, Luke tells us Jesus appeared to two of his disciples on the way to Emmaus and says to them,

"O foolish ones, and slow of heart to believe all that the prophets have spoken! Was it not necessary that the Christ should suffer these things and enter into his glory?" And beginning with Moses and all the Prophets, he interpreted to them in all the Scriptures the things concerning himself. (Luke 24:25-27)

And later, he says to another group of disciples,

"These are my words that I spoke to you while I was still with you, that everything written about me in the Law of Moses and the Prophets and the Psalms must be fulfilled." Then he opened their minds to understand the Scriptures, and said to them, "Thus it is written, that the Christ should suffer and on the third day rise from the dead, and that repentance and forgiveness of sins should be proclaimed in his name to all nations, beginning from Jerusalem. You are witnesses of these things." (Luke 24:44-48)

In his book *What is Biblical Theology?* James Hamilton writes, "The Bible's big story, this overarching narrative, is also built out of smaller stories. At the same time, the stories told in the Old Testament work together to set up a mystery resolved in Christ."[75]

For instance, in Psalm 16, we find these interesting verses:

---

[75] *What is Biblical Theology? A Guide to the Bible's Story, Symbolism, and Patterns* by James M. Hamilton Jr. (Crossway, 2014).

Therefore my heart is glad, and my whole being rejoices;
  my flesh also dwells secure.
For you will not abandon my soul to Sheol,
  or let your holy one see corruption. (Psalm 16:9-10)

In this Psalm, the narrator says God won't abandon him to "Sheol" or let "your holy one" see corruption. What this is saying is that God won't let the "holy one" die and rot in the grave; he won't see the corruption and decay of death. But King David, who wrote this Psalm, is long dead! Clearly, this passage can't be about David. The "holy one" of God is not David, but the future Messiah. This prophecy was fulfilled when Jesus, after his execution, was resurrected and exited the tomb.[76]

Peter lays this all out for a group of Jews in Acts 2:

Brothers, I may say to you with confidence about the patriarch David that he both died and was buried, and his tomb is with us to this day. Being therefore a prophet, and knowing that God had sworn with an oath to him that he would set one of his descendants on his throne, he foresaw and spoke about the resurrection of the Christ, that he was not abandoned to Hades,[77] nor did his flesh see corruption. This Jesus God raised up, and of that we all are witnesses. (Acts 2:29-30)

Later, Peter explains all this again to some others, and he even quotes Psalm 16:10.[78]

In **Isaiah 52:13-53:12**, we have the famous prophecy about who is often called, "The Suffering Servant." Michael Brown, who is a Jewish convert to Christianity and holds a Ph.D. in Near Eastern Languages and Literatures, writes that Isaiah 52:13-53:12 is arguably "the clearest

---

[76] *Answering Jewish Objections to Jesus (Volume 3) Messianic Prophecy Objections* by Michael Brown (Baker Books, 2003).
[77] Sheol (Hebrew) = Hades (Greek) = The place of death, "the underworld."
[78] Acts 13:35-37.

prophecy of Jesus" and "one of the most important Messianic prophecies" in the entire Old Testament, and it "would not be exaggerating to say that more Jews have put their faith in Jesus as Messiah after reading this passage of Scripture than after reading any other passage."[79] Here are portions of that prophecy, written 700 years before Jesus of Nazareth walked the earth; the parallels between these passages and the life and death of Jesus for the forgiveness of sins are clear:

For he grew up before him like a young plant,
and like a root out of dry ground;
he had no form or majesty that we should look at him,
and no beauty that we should desire him.
He was despised and rejected by men;
a man of sorrows, and acquainted with grief;
and as one from whom men hide their faces
he was despised, and we esteemed him not.
Surely he has borne our griefs
and carried our sorrows;
yet we esteemed him stricken,
smitten by God, and afflicted.
But he was pierced for our transgressions;
he was crushed for our iniquities;
upon him was the chastisement that brought us peace,
and with his wounds we are healed.
All we like sheep have gone astray;
we have turned—every one—to his own way;
and the Lord has laid on him
the iniquity of us all. (Isaiah 53:2-6)

And they made his grave with the wicked
and with a rich man in his death,

---

[79]*Answering Jewish Objections to Jesus (Volume 3) Messianic Prophecy Objections* by Michael Brown (Baker Books, 2003).

although he had done no violence,
and there was no deceit in his mouth.
Yet it was the will of the Lord to crush him;
he has put him to grief;
when his soul makes an offering for guilt,
he shall see his offspring; he shall prolong his days;
the will of the Lord shall prosper in his hand.
Out of the anguish of his soul he shall see and be satisfied;
by his knowledge shall the righteous one, my servant,
make many to be accounted righteous,
and he shall bear their iniquities. (Isaiah 53:9-11)

Christmas in the Old (Yes, Old) Testament

As we look at Jesus' connection to the Old Testament, let's return to Jesus' birth again. In **Matthew 1:1**, Matthew calls Jesus *"the son of David, the son of Abraham"* and then goes on to give us Jesus' genealogy. This is important for Matthew's readers to know because all Jews knew the Messiah would be a descendent of Abraham and King David. Matthew is often called the "most Jewish" Gospel because Matthew is clearly concerned with showing that Jesus is the Jewish Messiah and the fulfillment of the Jewish Scripture.

Thus, to truly understand Jesus of Nazareth, we need to understand the Old Testament, and this is exactly why the writers of the New Testament constantly refer back to the Old Testament. In fact, Matthew does this more than any other Gospel writer.

When reading the Christmas story in **Matthew 1-2**, you'll notice that Matthew references the Old Testament four different times in this short narrative – four references to four different Old Testament prophets: Isaiah, Micah (with 2 Samuel), Hosea, and Jeremiah. But when we turn to the Old Testament to read these passages, we run into some problems: It's not so clear they're about Jesus!

So, let's look at these passages more closely and see what the Old Testament tells us about the first Christmas.

Matthew 2:15 / Hosea 11:1

After Jesus' birth, Joseph, Mary, and the newborn Jesus flee to Egypt to escape the persecution of Herod, and they would not return until after Herod's death. Matthew tells us this was to fulfill what God had spoken in **Hosea 11:1**:

"Out of Egypt I called my son."

Now, when we turn to Hosea 11:1 and read the context of the passage, we run into a problem: this passage isn't a prediction about Jesus! In fact, it's not about the Messiah at all! Hosea is clearly speaking about the nation of Israel, and the line "Out of Egypt I called my son" is clearly referring to the Exodus, when God liberated Israel from slavery under Pharaoh.

What's going on here? How does Jesus "fulfill" something not even about him?

Often, when we think of prophets and "fulfillment," we think of prophets making specific Nostradamus-like predictions about the future and those predictions coming true. Though these types of predictions do occur in the Bible, often this isn't the type of "fulfillment" the New Testament writers have in mind. What they have in mind is something called *typology*.

What is *typology*? Events, persons, or institutions that become patterns – that "echo" throughout God's redemptive history; these are called *types*. These types or patterns are seen throughout Scripture and foreshadow a future, ultimate fulfillment, called an *antitype*.

Who Jesus Ain't

For example, the Passover lamb and the Jewish sacrificial system are types that point forward to Jesus' sacrificial death for the sins of the world. Jesus' death (the antitype) fulfills the purpose of the Passover lamb and the Old Testament sacrifices (the types). Interestingly, Jesus was arrested and executed during the Jewish observation of the Passover.

When Matthew refers to Old Testament verses like Hosea 11:1 and says they were "fulfilled," he's speaking of typology. Here, he isn't saying Jesus fulfilled specific predictions about the Messiah, but that Jesus is the fulfillment of a pattern seen throughout God's redemptive plan. After all, as we looked at before, Jesus says in **Matthew 5:17,**

"Do not think that I have come to abolish the Law or the Prophets; I have not come to abolish them but to fulfill them."

To illustrate, Israel is often referred to as "God's son," but Jesus is considered the true Israel because he's God's true Son. Just like God liberated Israel from slavery in Egypt, Matthew is telling us that Jesus is the new Exodus, because through Jesus, God will liberate us from our slavery to sin. Scholar R.T. France writes in his commentary on Matthew that the Exodus is a powerful symbol of "the even greater work of deliverance" which God will accomplish through Jesus Christ.[80]

What Matthew is doing by using these Old Testament passages is pointing us to the prophets' larger message. This connection to the larger story of the Bible wouldn't have been lost on his original Jewish audience as it is often lost on us today. Usually, we're only looking at the little details; we want to know how this *one* New Testament verse fulfills this *one* Old Testament verse, yet we miss the big picture Matthew is painting.

[80] *The Gospel of Matthew* (The New International Commentary on the New Testament) by R. T. France (William B. Eerdmans Publishing Company, 2007).

Who Jesus Ain't

Matthew 2:18 / Jeremiah 31:15

Now, let's keep in mind what was just said about typology and fulfillment as we look at Matthew's use of **Jeremiah 31:15**:

"A voice was heard in Ramah,
weeping and loud lamentation,
Rachel weeping for her children;
she refused to be comforted, because they are no more."

Matthew uses this Old Testament reference after he reports that Herod killed all of the male children ages two-years-old and younger in Bethlehem. Again, we run into a similar problem as before: This section of Jeremiah is about the Babylonian exile; it has nothing to do with the Messiah! The Babylonian Empire had conquered Jerusalem and destroyed their Temple, and now the Jews were being deported to Babylon. This is a catastrophic event for the Jewish people. What's worse is that they brought it upon themselves. Since their rebellion against God had become so great, God withdrew his protection and allowed this to happen to Israel.

Typologically, we can say the suffering of children due to evil is certainly a pattern we see in Scripture. But is Matthew pointing us to Jeremiah to make a bigger point? I certainly think so: Despite the messages of God's judgment and wrath, this section of Jeremiah isn't one of gloom and punishment, but one of hope and restoration. I recommend you read the whole chapter of **Jeremiah 31** to see. But if nothing else, take note that shortly after the verse Matthew quotes, we're told of the coming *"new covenant" (31:31)* where God *"...will put my law within them, and I will write it on their hearts. And I will be their God, and they shall be my people... For I will forgive their iniquity, and I will remember their sin no more." (31:33-34)*

Who Jesus Ain't

<u>Matthew 2:6 / Micah 5:2/ 2 Samuel 5:2</u>

Matthew Chapter 2 begins with the story of the magi, who come looking for the new king of the Jews. When they inquire in Jerusalem, Herod goes to the chief priests and scribes and asks where this new king will be born. Matthew tells us:

They told him, 'In Bethlehem of Judea, for so it is written by the prophet:
"'And you, O Bethlehem, in the land of Judah,
are by no means least among the rulers of Judah;
for from you shall come a ruler
who will shepherd my people Israel.'" (Matthew 2:5-6)

Finally, we have a plain, undeniable prediction about the future Messiah! This passage, taken from Micah 5:2 (written 700 years before Jesus' birth), clearly speaks of a future leader coming from Bethlehem in Judea. Jews understood Micah 5:2 to be about the Messiah. Also, the Jews believed the Messiah would come from the tribe of Judah:

The scepter shall not depart from Judah,
nor the ruler's staff from between his feet,
until tribute comes to him;
and to him shall be the obedience of the peoples. (Genesis 49:10)

But is there even more to this reference to the Old Testament in Matthew than that?

The chief priests' and scribes' response to Herod isn't a direct, word-for-word quote, but a "loose" quote, which is more of a paraphrase with some interpretation thrown in. This is the sort of thing pastors commonly do today while teaching, and we see these Jewish teachers doing it here. Further, the chief priests and scribes don't just cite Micah 5:2, but their response is also taken from **2 Samuel 5:2**:

Who Jesus Ain't

And the LORD said to you, 'You shall be shepherd of my people Israel, and you shall be prince over Israel.'

If we read farther in Micah past 5:2, we also see this theme of the Messiah being a shepherd of his people:

But you, O Bethlehem Ephrathah,
  who are too little to be among the clans of Judah,
from you shall come forth for me
  one who is to be ruler in Israel,
whose coming forth is from of old,
  from ancient days.
Therefore he shall give them up until the time
  when she who is in labor has given birth;
then the rest of his brothers shall return
  to the people of Israel.
And he shall stand and shepherd his flock in the strength of the LORD,
  in the majesty of the name of the LORD his God.
And they shall dwell secure, for now he shall be great
  to the ends of the earth. (Micah 5:2-4)

It's safe to say that when most people think of the Old Testament prophets, they think of messages of doom and gloom for Israel, but often – maybe even more than we realize – during their tirades we find messages of a future hope. Often these messages of hope include a promise of God's future restoration of his people, protection for his faithful remnant, and sometimes even words about a mysterious future leader.

Micah 5 speaks of this new ruler and a new peace. He will be born in Bethlehem (like Jesus) and from the tribe of Judah (like Jesus) and he will come from *"of old, from ancient days,"*[81] an undeniable reference to the eternal existence of God.[82]

Matthew 1:23 / Isaiah 7:14

To end, we come to perhaps the most hotly debated prophecy in the Bible. Matthew tells us Mary, an unwed virgin, finds herself *"to be with child from the Holy Spirit,"*[83] and Matthew quotes **Isaiah 7:14**, telling us:

"All this took place to fulfill what the Lord had spoken by the prophet:
'Behold, the virgin shall conceive and bear a son,
and they shall call his name Immanuel'
(which means, God with us)."

Some of the controversy concerning Matthew's use of Isaiah 7:14 has to do with the word "virgin." In the ancient Hebrew of Isaiah, the word could be translated "young woman." A young woman is not particularly a virgin, some argue; yet, it's a weak argument since the word is understood to refer to an unmarried, sexually chaste maiden.

Moreover, why would Isaiah not write the much more commonly-used Hebrew words for "woman" if there was nothing unique about his woman? Instead, he chose to use a word scholar R.T. France describes as "unusual" and rarely used in the Old Testament.[84] Furthermore, Matthew clearly shows us how Jesus' first followers understood the word because in his Gospel he uses the Greek word that undeniably means "virgin"!

---

[81] Micah 5:2.

[82] Also see Daniel 7:9.

[83] Matthew 1:18.

[84] *The Gospel of Matthew* (The New International Commentary on the New Testament) by R. T. France.

But there's another problem with Matthew's use of Isaiah 7:14. This passage doesn't seem to be about the far future; the "son" which is to come seems to be coming during the time period of Isaiah's writing. Frankly, the passage is perplexing. If the "son" was to come soon after the writing of Isaiah, who from Jewish history could it possibly be? Yet, again, our understanding of *typology* can help us here: If this passage does, in fact, refer to a child other than the Messiah, this child is a foreshadowing of the future Christ.

If this isn't a satisfying answer for you, then we only have to ask again, *Why does Matthew point us to this particular Scripture?* We only have to read a little farther in Isaiah to Chapter 9 to find out. Here, we again come across a child born, and this time it's clear whom this child is:

"For to us a child is born,
to us a son is given;
and the government shall be upon his shoulder,
and his name shall be called
Wonderful Counselor, Mighty God,
Everlasting Father, Prince of Peace." (Isaiah 9:6)

In With the New, But Not Out With the Old

Where looking at the messianic prophecies are always intriguing, there are plainer, more obvious reasons that understanding the Old Testament leads to a better understanding of Jesus and the New Testament. In the Old Testament, we learn of God creating the world "good"[85] and then mankind's fall into sin, which brought the curse of death on all of creation.[86] Throughout the Old Testament, we see God reveals himself to Israel, his chosen people to represent him on the

---

[85] Genesis 1.
[86] Genesis 3.

earth, who were to bless the world, yet we see how they always fall short and stray from the God of their salvation. But all the while, God is still preparing the world for the redemption of his creation, and this leads us into the New Testament. This plan of redemption culminates when God the Son becomes flesh and dies as a sacrifice for the sins of the world.

You can't completely understand the New Testament without understanding the Old Testament. Like many Christians, when I started reading the Bible on my own, I jumped to the New Testament and started with the Gospels about Jesus. But as I've gained a better understanding of the Old Testament over time, I've come to understand Jesus so much better. Not only did I start to become familiar with more of the allusions to the Old Testament Jesus makes, but I also became aware just how much Jesus and the New Testament writers refer back to the Old Testament – and it's a lot! When you realize this, it motivates you to work for a better grasp of the Old Testament. If Jesus found the Old Testament so important, then there must be a reason.

Conversely, understanding the New Testament helps us to interpret the Old Testament. Graeme Goldsworthy writes, "The gospel will interpret the Old Testament by showing us its goal and meaning. The Old Testament will increase our understanding of the gospel by showing us what Christ fulfills... Every word in Scripture points to Jesus and finds its meaning in him."[87]

To be honest, the Old Testament is a much more difficult read than the New Testament for many people. The Old Testament is longer with sections that are perplexing and difficult to get through. People who try to read the Bible from front to back often never even get through the

[87] Chapter 5:"We Know Him Through Scripture" & Chapter 6:"The Bible Is the Divine-Human Word" from *According to Plan: The Unfolding Revelation of God in the Bible* by Graeme Goldsworthy.

Old Testament and, thus, never make it to the Gospels and Jesus. Since I'm a Christian because of Jesus Christ, I recommend to people who are reading the Bible for the first time to read the Old and New Testaments simultaneously. So, for example, read two chapters of Genesis and then two chapters of Matthew, and so on. Also, a good study Bible – like the ESV and NIV study Bibles – will be a great help in understanding the more perplexing parts.

Remember, the first Christians were Jews. If God were doing something new – and these Jews certainly believed God was doing something new through Jesus of Nazareth – they would expect new Scripture to come with this new divine work.[88] When we get into the New Testament, that's exactly what we have. We have the writings of Jesus' apostles – men who were witnesses of Jesus' ministry and resurrection and appointed by Jesus of Nazareth himself.

Within the New Testament, we see confirmation that Jesus' apostles considered their teachings from God. Paul writes in one of his letters,

For I would have you know, brothers, that the gospel that was preached by me is not man's gospel. For I did not receive it from any man, nor was I taught it, but I received it through a revelation of Jesus Christ. (Galatians 1:11-12)[89]

The apostles believed they were passing on the message – the gospel, the good news – of Jesus, who they believed was God in the flesh. So strongly did Paul believe this, he's motivated to say this to those turning away from Jesus' teachings for false teachings:

I am astonished that you are so quickly deserting him who called you in the grace of Christ and are turning to a different gospel— not that

---

[88] *The Heresy of Orthodoxy* by Andreas Kostenberger and Michael Kruger. See Chapter 7.

[89] Also see 1 Thessalonians 2:13.

there is another one, but there are some who trouble you and want to distort the gospel of Christ. But even if we or an angel from heaven should preach to you a gospel contrary to the one we preached to you, let him be accursed. As we have said before, so now I say again: If anyone is preaching to you a gospel contrary to the one you received, let him be accursed. (Galatians 1:6-9)

And, immediately afterwards, Paul makes it clear he's not concerned with what men think:

For am I now seeking the approval of man, or of God? Or am I trying to please man? If I were still trying to please man, I would not be a servant of Christ. (Galatians 1:10)

Not only that, but the apostles understood the writings of the other apostles as Scripture. Paul writes in **1 Timothy 5:18**,

For the Scripture says, "You shall not muzzle an ox when it treads out the grain," and, "The laborer deserves his wages."

Paul quotes two lines here, calling both Scripture. The first is from **Deuteronomy 25:4** from the Old Testament, but the second quote is Jesus' words. These words of Jesus' are recorded in both **Luke 10:7** and **Matthew 10:10**. Here we have Paul – a Jew brought up to strictly follow God's Word, educated under Gamaliel (one of the most respected rabbis of his day) and trained as a Pharisee[90] – putting the words of Jesus and the Gospels of Luke and Matthew on the same level as the divine Jewish Scripture!

Furthermore, we have Peter – Jesus' most prominent disciple and "rock"[91] – in one of his letters referring to Paul's letters as Scripture:

---

[90] Acts 22:3; Philippians 3:5.
[91] Matthew 16:15-18.

And count the patience of our Lord as salvation, just as our beloved brother Paul also wrote to you according to the wisdom given him, as he does in all his letters when he speaks in them of these matters. There are some things in them that are hard to understand, which the ignorant and unstable twist to their own destruction, as they do the other Scriptures. (2 Peter 3:15-16)

The Bible didn't fall out of the sky. Christians believe men through whom the Holy Spirit worked wrote it. So, the Bible is written by men, but it is from God. From Jesus' own words to his disciples, we get a clue as to how the New Testament was divinely written:

But the Helper, the Holy Spirit, whom the Father will send in my name, he will teach you all things and bring to your remembrance all that I have said to you. (John 14:26)

I still have many things to say to you, but you cannot bear them now. When the Spirit of truth comes, he will guide you into all the truth, for he will not speak on his own authority, but whatever he hears he will speak, and he will declare to you the things that are to come. (John 16:12-13)

The writers of the New Testament themselves also give us some insight into how the Christian Scriptures came to be. Peter writes in one of his letters,

For we did not follow cleverly devised myths when we made known to you the power and coming of our Lord Jesus Christ, but we were eyewitnesses of his majesty. For when he received honor and glory from God the Father, and the voice was borne to him by the Majestic Glory, "This is my beloved Son, with whom I am well pleased,"[92] we ourselves heard this very voice borne from heaven, for we were with

---

[92] Peter is talking about "The Transfiguration" of Jesus, of which he was an eyewitness. See Matthew 17:1–9, Mark 9:2-8, Luke 9:28–36.

him on the holy mountain. And we have the prophetic word more fully confirmed, to which you will do well to pay attention as to a lamp shining in a dark place, until the day dawns and the morning star rises in your hearts, knowing this first of all, that no prophecy of Scripture comes from someone's own interpretation. For no prophecy was ever produced by the will of man, but men spoke from God as they were carried along by the Holy Spirit. (2 Peter 1:16-21)

Peter says a lot here; we're not going to unpack it all, but he says that his and the other apostles' message isn't based on made-up stories ("cleverly devised myths") but on their eyewitness testimony and the certainty of Scripture ("the prophetic word"), and that Scripture comes not from man alone, but from men speaking things from God through the power of the Holy Spirit.

Furthermore, Luke begins his Gospel by explaining to someone named Theophilus how he investigated the events written about in his Gospel:

Inasmuch as many have undertaken to compile a narrative of the things that have been accomplished among us, just as those who from the beginning were eyewitnesses and ministers of the word have delivered them to us, it seemed good to me also, having followed all things closely for some time past, to write an orderly account for you, most excellent Theophilus, that you may have certainty concerning the things you have been taught. (Luke 1:1-4)

So, the New Testament record is a combination of eyewitness testimony, careful investigation, and divine guidance. Moreover, Paul reminds the readers of his letters that the apostles' message, given to them by God, has been confirmed by "signs and wonders," meaning miracles:

The signs of a true apostle were performed among you with utmost patience, with signs and wonders and mighty works.
(2 Corinthians 12:12)

Who Jesus Ain't

It was declared at first by the Lord, and it was attested to us by those who heard, while God also bore witness by signs and wonders and various miracles and by gifts of the Holy Spirit distributed according to his will. (Hebrews 2:3-4)

Yes, it wasn't just Jesus who performed miracles according to the New Testament, but also his first disciples, which we see explicitly in the Book of Acts. Jesus' first followers spoke languages they never knew,[93] healed cripples[94] and paralytics,[95] drove out demons,[96] even brought people back to life,[97] and one survived the bite of a venomous snake![98] We're told in Acts:

And awe came upon every soul, and many wonders and signs were being done through the apostles. (Acts 2:43) [99]

Also in Acts, after proclaiming Jesus' resurrection and explaining his own miraculous conversion from a persecutor of Jesus-followers to a follower of Jesus himself, Paul is accused of being crazy. So, Paul announces before King Herod Agrippa II, his sister Bernice, and procurator Festus,

"I am not out of my mind, most excellent Festus, but I am speaking true and rational words. For the king knows about these things, and to him I speak boldly. For I am persuaded that none of these things has escaped his notice, for this has not been done in a corner. (Acts 26:25-26)

---

[93] Acts 2:1-13.
[94] Acts 3:1-10.
[95] Acts 9:32-35.
[96] Acts 16:16-18.
[97] Acts 9:36-43; 20:7-12.
[98] Acts 28:3-6.
[99] Also see Acts 5:12, 19:11-12.

Who Jesus Ain't

Just as the Jewish Scriptures are clearly important to the early Christians, most of whom were Jews, the early Christian church valued the New Testament as the written word of God as well. In fact, God's written word was so important to the first Christians, many historians believe Christians invented the codex. The codex is the early ancestor to our modern, post-printing press books. Writings used to be done on scrolls, which were long and bulky, and not only difficult to carry, but burdensome in handling when looking for specific passages. A codex, like our modern books, was bound on one edge of the papyrus paper and could be leafed through and carried much more easily. Even if historians aren't 100% certain that Christians invented the codex, they're certain that Christians were the first to widely use and popularize the codex.[100]

Likewise, six hundred years after Jesus' earthly ministry, in the Quran, Mohammad refers to Jews and Christians as "The People of the Book." Written Scripture is what separated Jews and Christians from their pagan neighbors, and this is why 2,000 years after Jesus walked the earth we can still follow the same faith Jesus' first disciples followed: because we have a written record by Jesus' apostles themselves that has been preserved and passed down to us. Scripture – both the Old and New Testaments – are absolutely essential to the Christian identity – it always has been.

In Chapter 3 of this book, we saw why we can be confident that the New Testament has been accurately preserved over the centuries, and in this chapter we saw why we can trust the Old Testament. In fact, Jesus himself gave us assurance of this when he said,

---

[100] *The Heresy of Orthodoxy* by Andreas Kostenberger and Michael Kruger. See Chapter 7.

Heaven and earth will pass away, but my words will not pass away. (Matthew 24:35).[101]

---

[101] Chapter 14:"What Did Jesus Teach About the Bible?" in *I Don't Have Enough Faith To Be an Atheist* by Norman Geisler & Frank Turek was extremely helpful in composing sections of this chapter.

CHAPTER 7: JESUS AIN'T A MYTH OR LEGEND PART 1

Despite the New Testament being the most reliable and corroborated historical document from ancient times, why is it viewed with such skepticism when other much less reliable ancient documents are rarely questioned? If Jesus is the most well-documented person in the ancient world, why do people still claim he's a myth? If the same skepticism that's applied towards Jesus were applied to other ancient figures, we'd have to accept that we know nearly nothing about the ancient world!

As I said before, often people's rejection of Jesus and the New Testament has nothing to do with the quality of the evidence, but a view of the world that rejects God and the supernatural.

Who Jesus Ain't

But for the sake of argument, let's do away with the Bible and ask, *Is there evidence that Jesus wasn't a myth or legend?*

There are at least 10 ancient, non-Christian sources that mention Jesus of Nazareth. All are dated after the New Testament, so the New Testament is still our best source for learning about Jesus, but to have information about Jesus from non-Christian sources is significant because the likeliness that the source writers would put a biased positive slant on the information about Jesus is slim. Likewise, if the information comes from someone actually *opposed* to Christianity, we can assume a biased negative slant is likely (at worst) or a neutral, unbiased view (at best). So, to have an opponent of Christianity confirm information that appears in the New Testament is significant (and exciting).

On the other hand, we have to be fair and honest and not make these sources say more (or less) than what they actually say. Some of the sources may not so much be saying something about Jesus directly (though some do), but reporting information about what ancient Christians believed about Jesus. Still, these are useful because they tell us important information about early Christianity. The one thing that becomes clear is that Christians considered Jesus God from early on, they were highly moral, and these Christians were willing to die for their belief that Jesus rose from the dead.

Here are 12 facts these ancient, non-Christian sources confirm, which are in harmony with the New Testament:

1. Jesus lived during the time of Tiberius Caesar.
2. He lived a virtuous life.
3. He was considered a wonder-worker.
4. He had a brother named James, who was killed for being a Christian.
5. Jesus was acclaimed to be the Messiah.
6. He was crucified under Pontius Pilate.

7. He was crucified on the eve of the Jewish Passover.
8. His disciples believed he rose from the dead.
9. His disciples were willing to die for their belief.
10. Christianity spread rapidly as far as Rome.
11. His disciples denied the Roman gods and worshiped Jesus as God.
12. After Jesus' execution, Christianity disappeared from public view briefly, but then abruptly grew.[102]

When you look at all of this information from the ancient, non-Christian sources together, it paints a picture that's quite compelling.

Of these ancient non-Christian sources, the following three are considered the best because they're the closest to the actual events and written by ancient historians who have been shown to be reliable:

Josephus, Jewish historian (written about 90-95 AD)

"At this time there was a wise man who was called Jesus. His conduct was good and he was known to be virtuous. And many people from among the Jews and the other nations became disciples. Pilate condemned him to be crucified and to die. But those who had become his disciples did not abandon his discipleship. They reported that he had appeared to them three days after his crucifixion, and that he was alive; accordingly he was perhaps the Messiah, concerning whom the prophets have recounted wonders."

---

[102] This list is adapted from the book *I Don't Have Enough Faith to Be an Atheist*, Chapter 9:"Do We Have Early Testimony About Jesus?" by Norman Geisler and Frank Turek. For more in-depth critiques of these ancient documents see *The Historical Jesus* by Gary Habermas (College Press Publishing Company, 1997, 2nd Ed.) and *The Jesus Legend* by Paul Rhodes Eddy and Gregory A. Boyd (Baker Academic, 2007).

Who Jesus Ain't

"Upon [procurator] Festus' death, Caesar sent Albinus to Judea as procurator. But before he arrived, King Agrippa had appointed Ananus to the priesthood... [He] was rash and followed the Sadducees, who are heartless when they sit judgment. Ananus thought that with Festus dead and Albinus still on the way, he would have his opportunity. Convening the judges of the Sanhedrin, he brought before them a man named James, the brother of Jesus, who was called Christ, and certain others. He accused them of having transgressed the law, and condemned them to be stoned to death."

Pliny, Roman senator (written about 111 AD)

"I have asked them if they are Christians, and if they admit it, I repeat the question a second and third time, with a warning of the punishment awaiting them. If they persist, I order them to be led away for execution; for, whatever the nature of their admission, I am convinced that their stubbornness and unshakable obstinacy ought not go unpunished... They also declared that the sum total of their guilt or error amounted to no more than this: they had met regularly before dawn on a fixed day to chant verses alternately amongst themselves in honor of Christ as if to a god, and also to bind themselves by oath, not for any criminal purpose, but to abstain from theft, robbery, and adultery... This made me decide it was all the more necessary to extract the truth by torture from two slave-women, whom they called deaconesses. I found nothing but a degenerate sort of cult carried to extravagant lengths."

Cornelius Tacitus, Roman proconsul & historian (written in 115 AD)

"Therefore, to stop the rumor [that the burning of Rome in 64 AD had taken place by his order], Nero fastened the guilt and inflicted the most exquisite tortures on a class hated for their abominations, called Christians by the populace. Christus [Christ], from whom the name had

its origin, suffered the extreme penalty during the reign of Tiberius at the hands of one of our procurators, Pontius Pilatus, and a most mischievous superstition, thus checked for the moment, again broke out not only in Judaea, the first source of the evil, but even in Rome, where all things hideous and shameful from every part of the world find their center and become popular. Accordingly, an arrest was first made of all who pleaded guilty: then, upon their information, an immense multitude was convicted, not so much of the crime of firing the city as of hatred against mankind. Mockery of every sort was added to their deaths. Covered with the skins of beasts, they were torn by dogs and perished, or were nailed to crosses, or were doomed to the flames and burnt, to serve as a nightly illumination, when daylight had expired."

Skeptics, of course, question these documents, especially Josephus' work, accusing Christians of corrupting Josephus' original words by adding to the manuscript. Some claim Josephus, a non-Christian Jew, would never write so favorably about Jesus. Others claim these were written after Jesus' lifetime, so they're based only on hearsay. My challenge to these skeptics, then, is for them to provide evidence for these claims. Christians are constantly asked, "Where's the evidence?" So, if these documents were doctored, where are the early manuscripts before the supposed corruptions? If these reliable historians decided to write based on hearsay, what proof do we have of this? Let's be fair; anyone can make a claim, but where's the evidence? Much is possible, but what is plausible based on the evidence?

Interestingly, at one time there only existed manuscripts of Josephus with slightly different phrasing that contained what seemed like additions that favored the Christian view of Jesus. Both Christian and non-Christian scholars were skeptical of specific words and phrases. Then, an earlier Arabic version was discovered without the questionable words and phrases, proving that scribes *had* added to the words of Josephus, *but* also confirming the authenticity of the Jesus passages.[103] There has never been any ancient manuscript of these writings of Josephus discovered that don't include the passages about Jesus or Jesus' brother James (or John the Baptist, who only appears elsewhere in the New Testament).

What Josephus writes is not contradictory to him being a non-Christian Jew. Josephus doesn't write that Jesus rose from the dead; he writes that Jesus' disciples reported that he rose from the dead. What Josephus is writing is a neutral report based on investigation. Josephus wrote this within the lifetime of people who would've witnessed the ministry of Jesus. The quote from the two Roman sources would've been written when people who were young during Jesus' ministry were still living.

What's interesting is that Josephus and Tacitus mention Jesus being put to death by Pontius Pilate. Despite this, some skeptics in the past have even challenged the claim that Pilate ever existed, not just Jesus. But in 1961 archaeologists found an inscription on a Roman building naming Pontius Pilate as the perfect (governor) of Judea. Tacitus, being part of the Roman elite himself, had easy access to records, and it would've been extremely sloppy historical writing for him to claim this real Roman leader executed a make-believe Jew.

Where someone dedicated to an atheistic, anti-supernatural worldview may still not accept all of the New Testament as fact, few (if any) familiar with the historical evidence would say Jesus never existed at all. Even Bart Ehrman, a former Christian turned skeptic, a New Testament scholar, and an author of several books attacking the traditional understanding of the Bible, says that "whatever else you may think about Jesus, he certainly did exist."[104]

---

[103] *The Jesus Legend* by Paul Rhodes Eddy and Gregory A. Boyd. See Chapter 4: "A Conspiracy of Silence."

[104] *Did Jesus Exist?: The Historical Argument for Jesus of Nazareth* by Bart Ehrman (HarperOne, 2012) and "Did Jesus Exist?" on huffingtonpost.com (2013-03-20).

Any Evidence Other than Writings?

The medieval Catholic Church claimed to have all sorts of archaeological artifacts belonging to Jesus and his apostles, but no one takes those seriously anymore – and with good reason. Frankly, if we had some artifacts that belonged to Jesus or archaeological evidence other than the documents mentioned above, I honestly don't think it would make a difference to a skeptic. I'm saying this as a former skeptic and atheist, and someone who still approaches everything with a good dose of skepticism. After all, we have 13 letters written by Paul himself and a thorough account of Paul's ministry in the book of Acts that spans about 30 years, including specific historical people and places, and still some skeptics claim he, like Jesus, never existed.

There are people who also disbelieve the first moon landing and the Jewish Holocaust and the deaths of Elvis, Osama bin Laden, and Tupac. To be clear, I'm perfectly aware that providing evidence for these modern events is much easier than for the life of an ancient rabbi, but my point is that some people make up their minds about things and, after that, no amount of evidence will dissuade them. Doubt can be cast upon everything if that's how we choose to approach things, and often skeptics question everything but their own skepticism.

Let's keep in mind, Jesus was a humble carpenter from the backwaters of the Roman Empire whose ministry only lasted three years, and he became the most famous and influential person in the history of the world. Whether a believer or a skeptic, that has to make you wonder about what sort of man he was. If Jesus hadn't risen from the dead, what could he have possibly done or said to motivate his original disciples to travel the ancient world proclaiming he had risen? And what possible reason did his disciples have – what did they possibly gain – by dying for this lie? Why would the disciples, as eyewitnesses (not extremist followers hundreds of years later), die for something they very well knew was a lie? Money, sex, or power couldn't have been motivators. Based on the historical evidence, they all died prematurely as moral, peaceful, and poor men.

History tells us there were men both before and after Jesus who claimed to be the Messiah. Let me ask you: Can you name any of them? Even one? Here's the reason the vast majority of us can't: Because they all met untimely deaths, many by the hands of the Romans, and after their deaths, their followers dispersed. The movement was over. Their self-proclaimed Messiah was dead. Yet, after Jesus' crucifixion, his followers grew rapidly and spread far and wide, radically changing the Roman Empire and the world. What can explain this?

As I said, there wasn't a lot of writing being done in the ancient world, and most of it had to do with kings and emperors and powerful men. A crucified criminal was a scorned, degraded affront to a Roman[105] and seen as cursed by God to a Jew.[106] Why would any Jew or Roman believe a story about a crucified man coming back to life? What Jew or Roman would radically change his life - turning his back on his culture and religion - to follow stories about a crucified criminal? The fact that we know anything about a rabbi from an insignificant region of the Roman Empire is amazing. The fact that much of the world knows the name of a crucified Messiah is unexplainable.

Tradition and history tell us of Jesus' original twelve disciples, eleven died violent deaths proclaiming that the God of Peace had come in the flesh and died for the sins of the world. The exception, the apostle John, was exiled to an island. The apostle Paul and Jesus' brother James were

---

[105] As thoroughly documented by Martin Hengel in *Crucifixion (In the Ancient World and the Folly of the Message of the Cross)*, (Facets Series, Fortress Press, 1977).

[106] Deuteronomy 21:23: "his body shall not remain all night on the tree, but you shall bury him the same day, for a hanged man is cursed by God. You shall not defile your land that the Lord your God is giving you for an inheritance."

also put to death proclaiming Jesus had risen and was Lord. You would think one of them would've piped up beforehand and said, "OK, we made it all up!"

Here's the thing: People die for their faith all of the time because – whether it is or not – they believe it's true. But the disciples of Jesus were in the unique position to know without a shadow of a doubt whether their faith was based on truth or a lie – and that was dependent on whether God rose Jesus from the grave or not. And no one willingly dies for something they know is a lie.

CHAPTER 8: JESUS AIN'T SCHIZOPHRENIC

It's common knowledge that Christians believe Jesus is God. But when someone is reading the New Testament for the first time, this idea that Jesus is God may cause some confusion:

- If Jesus is God, why is he called the Son of God?
- How can someone be both human and God? How does that possibly work?
- And if Jesus is God, why does he seem to talk so much as if God is someone else? In fact, we even see Jesus praying to God in the Gospels. If Jesus is God, to whom is he praying? Is he talking to himself? Is Jesus schizophrenic?

The Trinity: 3 Persons, 1 Nature

Before we get into Jesus being God in the flesh, it would be helpful to understand one of the most unique beliefs of Christianity and perhaps one of the harder ones to wrap our heads around: The Trinity.

The Trinity is defined as three persons sharing one divine nature. Christians believe in one God,[107] but that one God is three persons. Christians are not polytheists, believing in many gods. The Bible clearly teaches that there is only one, true God (and, thus, Christians are monotheists), but three persons – the Father, the Son, and the Holy Spirit – share that same divine identity. It's really not as difficult to understand as people make it out to be: Three distinct personalities share the same divine nature; therefore, they are one.

James White's definition of the Trinity in his book *The Forgotten Trinity* is clear and concise: "Within the one Being that is God, there exists eternally three coequal and coeternal persons, namely, the Father, the Son, and the Holy Spirit."[108] These three personalities are all equal in power and abilities, and they have always existed as such for all of eternity as one united being. White goes on to quote Hank Hanegraaff of the Christian Research Institute: "when speaking of the Trinity, we need to realize that we are talking about one *what* and three *who's*."

To understand the Trinity, it's best to state the doctrine in three sentences:

---

[107] For example, see Isaiah 43:10: "Before me no god was formed, nor shall there be any after me." And Isaiah 44:6: "I am the first and I am the last; besides me there is no god."

[108] *The Forgotten Trinity* by James White, Chapter 2: "What is the Trinity?" (Bethany House, 1998).

Who Jesus Ain't

1. **God is three persons – Father, Son, and Holy Spirit.**
2. **Each person is fully God.**
3. **There is only one God.**

Denying or changing any of these three statements would not accurately illustrate the biblical belief of the Trinity. Moreover, trying to explain the Trinity in any other manner tends to lead to misrepresentations of the Trinity (and even heresy). Likewise, any analogy or illustration to explain the Trinity often proves misleading or inaccurate. As James White states in his book, "If something is truly unique, it cannot be compared to anything else, at least not without introducing some element of error."

The Trinitarian nature of God has several implications. In the book *Total Truth*, Nancy Pearcey writes of one of them:

> "The human race was created in the image of God, who is three Persons so intimately related as to constitute one Godhead... both oneness and threeness are equally real, equally ultimate, equally basic and integral to God's nature...

> "The balance of unity and diversity in the Trinity gives a model for human social life, because it implies that both individuality and relationship exist within the Godhead itself. God is being-in-communion. Humans are made in the image of a God who is a tri-unity — whose very nature consists in reciprocal love and communication among the Persons of the Trinity... the Trinity implies the dignity and uniqueness of individual persons. Over against radical individualism, the Trinity implies that relationships are not created by sheer choice but are built into the very essence of human nature. We are

not atomistic individuals but are created for relationships."[109]

Understanding that God has always existed as three persons in perfect unity and perfect relationship gives us insight into the biblical truth that *"God is love" (1 John 4:8).*

One thing the Bible certainly does *not* teach about the Trinity is that God existed as Father, Son, and Holy Spirit at different times. This is an old heresy called *Modalism*. Modalism teaches that God was the Father at one time in history, and then he ceased to be the Father and became the Son, and then later he ceased to be the Son and became the Holy Spirit. If this were the case, Jesus is certainly schizophrenic because we see him praying to God the Father throughout the Gospels. If Modalism is true, who is he talking to? Himself? All three persons of the Trinity have always existed, and they have always existed together. We clearly see this at Jesus' baptism:

And when Jesus was baptized, immediately he went up from the water, and behold, the heavens were opened to him, and he saw the Spirit of God descending like a dove and coming to rest on him; and behold, a voice from heaven said, "This is my beloved Son, with whom I am well pleased." (Matthew 3:16-17)

Here, we see the complete Trinity all acting at the same moment in time: Jesus (God the Son in the flesh) is being baptized. God the Holy Spirit ("the Spirit of God") descends to him. And God the Father speaks from Heaven.

We also see the Trinity plainly stated by Jesus in Matthew 28:

---

[109] *Total Truth: Liberating Christianity From Its Cultural Captivity,* Chapter 4:"Surviving the Spiritual Wasteland" by Nancy Pearcey (Crossway, 2004).

Who Jesus Ain't

Go therefore and make disciples of all nations, baptizing them in the name of the Father and of the Son and of the Holy Spirit (Matthew 28:19)

The important thing to notice here is that Jesus says to baptize in the *name* (singular), not *names* (plural), of the Father, Son, and Holy Spirit. Here, we have three distinct persons with one shared "name" – one shared identity, one shared divine nature. Thus, in **John 1:1**, we are told,

In the beginning was the Word, and the Word was with God, and the Word was God.

The context of the rest of John 1 lets us know that "the Word" is referring to God the Son (who becomes Jesus, God the Son in the flesh). Thus, God the Son can be described as being both "with" God and "was" God – *with* God *but also* God himself.

Throughout the Gospels, we see Jesus, God the Son, interacting with God the Father. For example, in the Garden of Gethsemane, before his arrest and crucifixion, he prays,

"Abba, Father, all things are possible for you. Remove this cup from me. Yet not what I will, but what you will." (Mark 14:36)

And in **John 17**, Jesus prays a long prayer to God the Father:

When Jesus had spoken these words, he lifted up his eyes to heaven, and said, "Father, the hour has come; glorify your Son that the Son may glorify you, since you have given him authority over all flesh, to give eternal life to all whom you have given him. And this is eternal life, that they know you the only true God, and Jesus Christ whom you have sent. I glorified you on earth, having accomplished the work that you gave me to do. And now, Father, glorify me in your own presence with the glory that I had with you before the world existed... (17:1-5)

Who Jesus Ain't

"I do not ask for these only, but also for those who will believe in me through their word, that they may all be one, just as you, Father, are in me, and I in you, that they also may be in us, so that the world may believe that you have sent me... (17:20-21)

"Father, I desire that they also, whom you have given me, may be with me where I am, to see my glory that you have given me because you loved me before the foundation of the world. O righteous Father, even though the world does not know you, I know you, and these know that you have sent me. I made known to them your name, and I will continue to make it known, that the love with which you have loved me may be in them, and I in them." (17:24-26)

Notice how the Son was with the Father even before the creation of all things, sharing mutually in glory as God, and notice also the intimacy and oneness the Father and Son share (*"you, Father, are in me, and I in you"*) though they are separate persons. In the same way, we see Jesus speaking about the Holy Spirit as a person unique from him:

"If you love me, you will keep my commandments. And I will ask the Father, and he will give you another Helper, to be with you forever, even the Spirit of truth, whom the world cannot receive, because it neither sees him nor knows him. You know him, for he dwells with you and will be in you. (John 14:15-17)

Notice the Holy Spirit, "the Spirit of Truth," is "another Helper," different from Jesus, and this third person of the Trinity will actually dwell in Jesus' followers. Shortly afterwards, Jesus also says this,

These things I have spoken to you while I am still with you. But the Helper, the Holy Spirit, whom the Father will send in my name, he will teach you all things and bring to your remembrance all that I have said to you. (John 14:25-26)

Nevertheless, I tell you the truth: it is to your advantage that I go away, for if I do not go away, the Helper will not come to you. But if I go, I will send him to you. And when he comes, he will convict the world concerning sin and righteousness and judgment: (John 16:7-8)

I still have many things to say to you, but you cannot bear them now. When the Spirit of truth comes, he will guide you into all the truth, for he will not speak on his own authority, but whatever he hears he will speak, and he will declare to you the things that are to come. He will glorify me, for he will take what is mine and declare it to you. (John 16:12-14)

A Modalist may point out that Jesus says in John 16:7-8 that he must go away in order for the Holy Spirit to come, but this is in no way the same as Jesus, God the Son, ceasing to exist and then becoming the Holy Spirit. Contrary to the Modalist view, Jesus says he will send the Holy Spirit and that the Holy Spirit will glorify him and take what is Jesus' and declare it to his followers. These are two separate persons of the Trinity working together. God the Son and God the Holy Spirit are one in nature but unique in personhood.

The Holy Spirit Ain't an "It"

This book is about Jesus of Nazareth, but let me take a moment to say something more about the Holy Spirit. The Holy Spirit is just as much God as the Father and the Son. As we saw above in Matthew 28, Jesus commands his disciples to baptize new believers in the name of the Holy Spirit, which is one with the Father and the Son, clearly putting the Holy Spirit on equal grounds with the Father and Son.

In the Book of Acts, we also find this:

But Peter said, "Ananias, why has Satan filled your heart to lie to the Holy Spirit and to keep back for yourself part of the proceeds of the land? While it remained unsold, did it not remain your own? And after it was sold, was it not at your disposal? Why is it that you have contrived this deed in your heart? You have not lied to man but to God." (Acts 5:3-4)

Notice, Peter first says Ananias lied to the Holy Spirit, and moments later he says Ananias lied to God. To Peter "God" and "the Holy Spirit" are interchangeable because they are one.

Further, the Holy Spirit is just as much a person as God the Father and God the Son. The Holy Spirit is not an "it." The Holy Spirit isn't the impersonal power of God or some impersonal force like Yoda uses in *Star Wars*. Notice in the Scripture below, the Holy Spirit is an "I" and "he," not an "it."

And while Peter was pondering the vision, the Spirit said to him, "Behold, three men are looking for you. Rise and go down and accompany them without hesitation, for I have sent them." (Acts 10:19-20)

While they were worshiping the Lord and fasting, the Holy Spirit said, "Set apart for me Barnabas and Saul for the work to which I have called them." (Acts 13:2)

And, once again, **John 16:13-15**:

[Jesus said,] "When the Spirit of truth comes, he will guide you into all the truth, for he will not speak on his own authority, but whatever he hears he will speak, and he will declare to you the things that are to come. He will glorify me, for he will take what is mine and declare it to you. All that the Father has is mine; therefore I said that he will take what is mine and declare it to you."

Finally, the following verses show the oneness of the Son and the Holy Spirit as God in that the Holy Spirit can also be referred to as "the Spirit of Jesus."

And they went through the region of Phrygia and Galatia, having been forbidden by the Holy Spirit to speak the word in Asia. And when they had come up to Mysia, they attempted to go into Bithynia, but the Spirit of Jesus did not allow them. (Acts 16:6-7)

1 Person, 2 Natures
(or: My Favorite Phrase I Learned in Seminary)

Before we look at what Jesus had to say about being God, there's one other thing that would be helpful to look into. Christians believe Jesus is both fully human and fully God. In seminary, I learned that Christian theologians call this the *hypostatic union*. (Isn't that a fantastic, elaborate phrase? Just take a moment and say it aloud a few times!)

Where the Trinity is *three persons* sharing *one divine nature*, Jesus is *one person* with *two natures*. By becoming Jesus of Nazareth, God the Son took on all that it is to be human, adding it to his divinity. God didn't change or lessen his divine nature by becoming a man; he added to it, taking on something new. Thus, Jesus (who is one person) has two natures: one human and one divine. Ladies and gentlemen, this is the wonder of the hypostatic union.

Of course, at this point, you're definitely wondering how Jesus can be both fully human and fully God. How exactly does that work? If Jesus is God, why when reading through the Gospels do we see Jesus as hungry? And tired? Why do we see him suffering? We even see him admitting that he doesn't know some things:

Who Jesus Ain't

Heaven and earth will pass away, but my words will not pass away. But concerning that day or that hour, no one knows, not even the angels in heaven, nor the Son, but only the Father. (Mark 13:31-32)

But I thought God knew everything?

The answer is found in **Philippians 2:6-8**:

[Jesus] who, though he was in the form of God, did not count equality with God a thing to be grasped, but emptied himself, by taking the form of a servant, being born in the likeness of men. And being found in human form, he humbled himself by becoming obedient to the point of death, even death on a cross.

Though Jesus is equal to God the Father and the Holy Spirit in all ways, he "emptied himself." Wayne Grudem in his *Systematic Theology*[110] is sure to point out that God the Son emptying himself doesn't mean that he gave up his divine attributes. Rather, the Son, who shared a special place of eminence in Heaven,[111] humbled himself and took a lowly status on Earth:

But whoever would be great among you must be your servant, and whoever would be first among you must be your slave, even as the Son of Man came not to be served but to serve, and to give his life as a ransom for many. (Matthew 20:26-28)

Jesus came to die for the sins of the world, and while doing so he also showed us how to live. This is why we see Jesus being baptized and praying and fasting and washing his disciples' feet[112] and modeling all the things that his followers should do. A true Christian, a true believer in Jesus Christ, follows Jesus' example.

---

[110] *Systematic Theology* by Wayne Grudem (Zondervan, 1994).
[111] John 17:5.
[112] John 13:1-17.

Who Jesus Ain't

When God the Son became flesh, becoming Jesus of Nazareth, he *voluntarily* submitted to the will of God the Father. This doesn't mean God the Son was no longer God, but he became dependent on the Father by his own choice. Thus, illustrating for us how we should live: in perfect obedience to God.

In **John 14**, as Jesus talks with his disciples, we see many instances of Jesus referring to his voluntary obedience and submission to the Father:

Do you not believe that I am in the Father and the Father is in me? The words that I say to you I do not speak on my own authority, but the Father who dwells in me does his works. (John 14:10)

And I will ask the Father, and he will give you another Helper [the Holy Spirit], to be with you forever. (John 14:16)

I will no longer talk much with you, for the ruler of this world [Satan] is coming. He has no claim on me, but I do as the Father has commanded me, so that the world may know that I love the Father. (John 14:30-31)

While walking the earth as Jesus of Nazareth, God the Son "humbled himself" by putting himself under God the Father's authority. The Father commands him; Jesus speaks with authority given to him by the Father; and he even asks the Father to send the Holy Spirit instead of doing it wholly on his own. Once you understand this, when Jesus says the following, it's not so shocking:

You heard me say to you, 'I am going away, and I will come to you.' If you loved me, you would have rejoiced, because I am going to the Father, for the Father is greater than I. (John 14:28)

Earlier in this chapter I emphasized how God is a Trinity of three persons, who are all completely equal in all ways, who are all completely and fully one God. So, how can Jesus say that the Father is greater than him? Because during his earthly ministry as Jesus of Nazareth, God the Son humbled himself.

To illustrate, it would be helpful to think of your boss at work. Your boss is human just like you, so you're equal as image-bearers of God in value, in deserving dignity, and in deserving certain self-evident rights. The fact that your boss is your boss and therefore has authority over you doesn't make him any more of a human being than you, nor does it make you any less of a human than him. Likewise, you may willingly submit to the authority of a judge or referee or teacher or parent or police officer, but it doesn't mean you're less than them in your identity as a human being. Though still divine and equal to God the Father in nature, God the Son gave up his rights as God for the love of his creation.

Hebrews 2:9 tells us,

But we see him who for a little while was made lower than the angels, namely Jesus, crowned with glory and honor because of the suffering of death, so that by the grace of God he might taste death for everyone.

And Paul in **2 Corinthians 8:9** writes,

For you know the grace of our Lord Jesus Christ, that though he was rich, yet for your sake he became poor, so that you by his poverty might become rich.

Let's All Thank Dr. Ware For a Helpful Illustration

Bruce Ware in his book *The Man Christ Jesus*[113] helps us understand how both the divine and human could function in one person.

---

[113] *The Man Christ Jesus: Theological Reflections on the Humanity of Christ* by Bruce Ware (Crossway, 2013).

Who Jesus Ain't

Speaking specifically about Jesus remaining sinless, Ware gives a helpful illustration to explain how this perceived tension between Jesus' human and divine natures played out. The idea is best understood by answering a question: *Why didn't the swimmer drown?*

In Ware's illustration, a swimmer is trying to break the world record for the longest continuous swim. For safety, he arranges for a boat to follow him. Thus, if he cramps or tires, he would be in no danger of drowning. But the swimmer breaks the record, never needing any assistance from the boat.

Now, why didn't the swimmer drown? Was it because of the boat? No, he didn't drown because he swam the whole time until he broke the record. To say he didn't drown because of the boat would be inaccurate. He never needed the boat!

Ware explains,

> "Although Christ was fully God, and as fully God he could not sin, he deliberately did not appeal, as it were, to his divine nature in fighting temptations that came to him. As a human, he not only could be tempted but was tempted in the greatest ways any human has been tempted in all of history. Yet for every temptation he faced, he fought and resisted fully and totally apart from any use of or appeal to his intrinsic divine nature...
> "Jesus did not sin, not because he relied on the supernatural power of his divine nature or because his divine nature overpowered his human nature, keeping him from sinning, but because he utilized all of the resources given to him in his humanity.

Who Jesus Ain't

> He loved and meditated on God's Word... he prayed
> to his Father; he trusted in the wisdom and rightness
> of his Father's will and Word; and, very significantly,
> he relied on the supernatural power of the Spirit to
> strengthen him to do all that he was called upon to
> do."[114]

In addition, Ware gives another helpful illustration:

"The point is this: the king cannot live according to all the rights and
privileges he knows as king while also living life, genuinely and
authentically, as a beggar... limitations of kingly expression are
necessary... [Jesus'] deity, while fully *possessed*, could not be fully
expressed..."[115]

As Jesus of Nazareth, God the Son willingly accepted the limitations of
the use of his divine attributes. Though he still possessed them, he made
use of them only by the authority of God the Father.

By first tackling these two hard biblical truths – the Trinity and Jesus'
dual nature – we're now more than ready to look at Jesus' divinity. The
idea that the Gospels teach that Jesus is God is so accepted in Christian
circles, it's difficult for Christians to believe that anyone would argue
otherwise. But some – including skeptics, Muslims, and Jehovah's
Witnesses – have argued Jesus never claimed to be God. And you have
to admit, when you read through the Gospels and nowhere see Jesus say
outright, "Hey, everyone, I'm God!" you may start to wonder: *Do they
have a point?* So, what did Jesus have to say about his divinity (or lack
of)? We'll explore this as we move to the next chapter.

---

[114] Chapter 5 in *The Man Christ Jesus* by Bruce Ware.

[115] Chapter 1 in *The Man Christ Jesus* by Bruce Ware.

CHAPTER 9: JESUS AIN'T A WISE MAN OR A GOOD MAN

Okay, maybe "Jesus Ain't a Wise Man or a Good Man" isn't the best title for this chapter. So, here's a more accurate chapter title: "Jesus Ain't *Just* a Wise Man or a Good Man." As we saw in the chapters before this one, Jesus was a real human who walked the earth, and – like all other humans – he was born, he had a family, and he had a childhood. Sometimes Christians focus on Jesus being God so much that they forget that Jesus was fully human as well, but the debate we come across more so today is that people try to make Jesus nothing but human.

Who Jesus Ain't

Did Jesus' First Followers Believe He was God?

When you read about Jesus in the four Gospels, you'll notice that his twelve disciples don't quite "get" who Jesus is.[116] Often times we find ourselves reading the Gospels, and we see the disciples misunderstanding Jesus or utterly amazed at something Jesus does, and we think "Hey! He's God in the flesh, you dummies! Why aren't you getting that?" But the reason we "get" it (and the disciples don't) is because we already know the rest of the story. Many people already know the story of Jesus *before* reading the Gospels, since he's arguably the most famous person ever to live. Conversely, the disciples were discovering who he was over the three years they spent with him. They didn't expect him to be God. Think about it! Even if you met the most caring, wise, and amazing person ever – even if he did some things that appeared miraculous – would you suspect he was God?

The disciples believed Jesus was the Messiah, the future king of Israel prophesied about in the Old Testament. But Jesus' followers never thought – nor did any Jews back then – that the Messiah would be God in the flesh.

Though Jesus' original twelve disciples didn't quite understand who Jesus was before, did they "get" that Jesus was God *after* his crucifixion and resurrection?

I think the answer is undeniably clear. John, one of Jesus' original twelve disciples, starts his gospel by referring to Jesus, God the Son, as "the Word" and telling us,

In the beginning was the Word, and the Word was with God, and the Word was God. (John 1:1)

So, Jesus, the Word, was both *with* God and *was* God. John also tell us,

---

[116] For example, see Luke 18:31-34; John 14:1-9; Matthew 8:23-27.

Who Jesus Ain't

And the Word became flesh and dwelt among us, and we have seen his glory, glory as of the only Son from the Father, full of grace and truth. (John 1:14)

The Word became a man by taking on flesh and lived among us, and then John goes on to tell us that this Word-Become-Flesh has shown us God:

No one has ever seen God; the only God, who is at the Father's side, he has made him known. (John 1:18)

It's safe to say John certainly understood Jesus to be God, sharing the divine nature with God the Father. Also note, here in John 1:18 (like in John 1:1), we see two persons of the Trinity: God the Son and God the Father, coexisting and one – so much so, John can even refer to Jesus as "the only God."

We see a proclamation of Jesus' divinity not only at the beginning of John's Gospel, but also at the end. Chapter 20 is the climatic ending of John's Gospel (Chapter 21 is the epilogue) where John closes his Gospel by telling us about Jesus' appearance to his disciple Thomas. Jesus had been crucified and buried in a tomb, but now some of his followers were claiming to have seen him alive. Thomas wasn't buying it. Essentially, he says unless he sees Jesus with his own eyes and touches him with his own hands, he won't believe that Jesus has overcome death. Then, when Thomas does see Jesus risen from the grave, he does believe, proclaiming,

My Lord and my God! (John 20:28)

What a fitting way for John to conclude his eyewitness account of the ministry of Jesus, by telling of Thomas' proclamation – a conclusion they had all reached when they encountered the risen Jesus: they were in the presence of God himself.

Let me ask you this: If Jesus were a good, honest, godly man but not God himself, wouldn't he have corrected Thomas? I know if anyone were so disoriented as to call me God, I would quickly correct them! We even see several followers of Jesus doing this in Scripture, like Paul and Barnabas when some pagans believe they're gods,[117] like Peter does when the Roman centurion Cornelius falls at his feet and worships

him,[118] and even angels.[119] When John, likely overcome with emotion, falls down to worship an angel, the angel says,

"You must not do that! I am a fellow servant with you and your brothers the prophets, and with those who keep the words of this book. Worship God." (Revelation 22:9)

James White brings up a good point about Thomas' proclamation: "No created being could *ever* allow such words to be addressed to him personally. No angel, no prophet, no sane human being, could ever allow himself to be addressed as 'Lord and God.' Yet Jesus not only accepts the words of Thomas but pronounces the blessing of faith upon them as well."[120]

Likewise, Jews and Christians alike agree that God alone is worthy of worship and to worship anything other than God is sin. Yet, after Jesus walks on water and calms a storm when his disciples are at danger at sea, we're told:

And those in the boat worshiped him, saying, "Truly you are the Son of God." (Matthew 14:33)

---

[117] Acts 14:14-15.

[118] Acts 10:25-26.

[119] Revelation 19:10 & 22:9.

[120] *The Forgotten Trinity*, Chapter 5:"Jesus Christ: God in Human Flesh" by James White.

Who Jesus Ain't

Does Jesus stop them? No. Jesus allows his disciples to worship him, an honor only allowed to God.

So, what else do the first followers of Jesus say about him?

Jesus Christ is *"God over all." (Romans 9:5)*

"He is the image of the invisible God, the firstborn of all creation. For by him all things were created, in heaven and on earth, visible and invisible, whether thrones or dominions or rulers or authorities – all things were created through him and for him. And he is before all things, and in him all things hold together. And he is the head of the body, the church. He is the beginning, the firstborn from the dead, that in everything he might be preeminent. For in him all the fullness of God was pleased to dwell…" (Colossians 1:15-19)

"For in him the whole fullness of deity dwells bodily." (Colossians 2:9)

Jesus is *"Christ, who is the image of God." (2 Corinthians 4:4)*

Jesus, *"who, although He existed in the form of God, did not regard equality with God a thing to be grasped, but emptied Himself, taking the form of a bond-servant, and being made in the likeness of men. Being found in appearance as a man, He humbled Himself by becoming obedient to the point of death, even death on a cross." (Philippians 2:6-8)*

"…our great God and Savior Jesus Christ" (Titus 2:13).

All of the above verses come from the apostle Paul's letters that are collected in the New Testament, all of which were written before the four Gospels. What does the rest of the New Testament have to say about Jesus' divinity?

Peter calls him *"our God and Savior Jesus Christ" (2 Peter 1:1).*

Who Jesus Ain't

Matthew writes that Jesus fulfilled the prophecy of **Isaiah 7:14**: *"God with us" (Matthew 1:13).*

Matthew 3:3 also tells us that John the Baptist, who prepared the way for Jesus, fulfills **Isaiah 40:3**, which reads,

A voice cries:
In the wilderness prepare the way of the LORD;
make straight in the desert a highway for our God.

The author of Hebrews says Jesus *"is the radiance of God's glory and the exact representation of his being, sustaining all things by his powerful word" (Hebrews 1:3)* and ascribes **Psalm 45:6** to Jesus:

But of the Son he says,
"Your throne, O God, is forever and ever,
the scepter of uprightness is the scepter of your kingdom. (Hebrews 1:8)

In **Acts 3:15**, Peter tells the men of Israel, *"You killed the author of life,"* which his Jewish audience would clearly understand to be referring to God, as anyone who has ever read the first chapter of the Bible would understand since God created everything from nothing.

Yes, Jesus' first followers certainly understood him to be God in the flesh.

Did Jesus Claim to Be God?

But what about Jesus himself? Did he claim to be God? Or did his first followers simply decide later that Jesus was God?

Who Jesus Ain't

JOHN 8

In John 8, Jesus is having a debate with some other Jews, and we find this perplexing exchange:

[Jesus said, "]Your father Abraham rejoiced that he would see my day. He saw it and was glad." So the Jews said to him, "You are not yet fifty years old, and have you seen Abraham?" Jesus said to them, "Truly, truly, I say to you, before Abraham was, I am." So they picked up stones to throw at him... (John 8:56-59)

What's going on here? Why the heck did the other Jews suddenly decide to pick up stones to stone Jesus to death? And what's with Jesus' strange grammar? Shouldn't he have said, "before Abraham was, I *was*," not "before Abraham was, I *am*"?

Abraham, who we find way back in Genesis, the first book of the Bible, lived hundreds of years before Jesus walked the earth; he's the father of the ancient Jewish nation of Israel. Abraham saw Jesus' "day," according the Jesus here. Essentially, Jesus is claiming that Abraham knew of his coming through God and was glad about it. The Jews, not understanding what Jesus is talking about, point out that Jesus is not even fifty years old: so how could he claim Abraham had seen him since Abraham was long, long dead?

Jesus replies in an unusual way: "before Abraham was, I am" and the Jews pick up stones to kill him. And again, we're left asking: Why?

To find the answer, we have to go back to the second book of the Bible, Exodus. In Exodus, God appears to Moses for the first time in the burning bush and tells him he wants Moses to lead Israel out of slavery in Egypt, and they have this exchange:

Then Moses said to God, "If I come to the people of Israel and say to them, 'The God of your fathers has sent me to you,' and they ask me,

Who Jesus Ain't

'What is his name?' what shall I say to them?" God said to Moses, "I AM WHO I AM." (Exodus 3:13-14)

This simple statement by God is actually loaded with significance. By saying "I AM WHO I AM," God isn't giving a name so much as a description of himself; he's giving an explanation of his being. Since there's no worldly thing to compare him to – he is beyond any comparison – God simply states, "I AM WHO I AM." In other words: I am self-existent and self-sufficient; I am the Uncaused First Cause; I am the only Necessary Being; I am the always-existing, uncreated, endlessly powerful creator of all things, and there's nothing else like me.

But God goes on to say something that gives us the answer to our question about the exchange between Jesus and the other Jews in John 8:

And he said, "Say this to the people of Israel, 'I AM has sent me to you.'" (Exodus 3:14)

Did you catch that? God told Moses to tell Israel that "I AM" has sent him. I AM is the name God gave to Moses when Moses asked for his name. Let's look at it again:

Then Moses said to God, "If I come to the people of Israel and say to them, 'The God of your fathers has sent me to you,' and they ask me, 'What is his name?' what shall I say to them?" God said to Moses, "I AM WHO I AM." And he said, "Say this to the people of Israel, 'I AM has sent me to you.'" (Exodus 3:13-14)

"I AM" translated from Hebrew is pronounced "Yahweh." Hebrew doesn't have vowels, so it's literally "YHWH." When you see "LORD" in all caps in your English-language Bible, the original Hebrew reads "YHWH," the name of God as given to Moses in Exodus 3:14.

So, why do the Jews decide to stone Jesus in John 8 for saying, "before Abraham was, I am"? Because they recognize that by saying "I AM," he is claiming to be God! Claiming to be God is blasphemy, and blasphemy in Israel was punishable by death by stoning.[121]

So, did Jesus claim to be God? Yes. By referring to himself as I AM, he did. And the Jews of his day recognized this, so much so they were ready to kill him for it.

JOHN 14

During the Last Supper on the night before Jesus was crucified, he gave his twelve disciples some very bad news: He told them that one of them would betray him; he told them Peter, the chief disciple, would deny knowing him three times; and Jesus told them he's going somewhere where they can't follow him.

These men have traveled with Jesus for three years – hearing his teachings, watching his miracles – and they're utterly convinced that he's the Messiah, the Christ – the one who will liberate Israel, the one sent by God and prophesied about in their Scripture. And now he's telling them all this. You can imagine what they were feeling: utterly demoralized, utterly deflated, and utterly defeated.

But then we come to **John 14:1-8**, and Jesus says this to them:

"Let not your hearts be troubled. Believe in God: believe also in me. In my Father's house are many rooms. If it were not so, would I have told you that I go to prepare a place for you? And if I go and prepare a place for you, I will come again and will take you to myself, that where I am you may be also. And you know the way to where I am going."

---

[121] Leviticus 24:16.

Who Jesus Ain't

Thomas said to him, "Lord, we do not know where you are going. How can we know the way?"

As we discussed before, often Jesus' disciples misunderstand him or totally don't understand what he's saying at all. Earlier, when Jesus said he was going someplace where they wouldn't be able to follow him, he was talking about his death on the cross for the forgiveness of the sins of the world (something only Jesus could accomplish). Now, in John 14, Jesus is talking about the afterlife, but Thomas doesn't get it. He neither understands where Jesus is going nor how they can know the way there. So, Jesus explains:

"I am the way, and the truth, and the life. No one comes to the Father except through me. If you had known me, you would have known my Father also. From now on you do know him and have seen him."
Philip said to him, "Lord, show us the Father, and it is enough for us."

Again, the disciples aren't understanding what Jesus is saying, so Philip decides to give Jesus an "easy" out – show us God the Father and it will be enough for them. In other words, Philip is saying, "Look, Jesus, I don't understand what you're talking about, but if you show us God, it's enough for me. I'll trust you." So, Philip is saying to Jesus: Show us God. How does Jesus respond?

Jesus said to him, "Have I been with you so long, and you still do not know me, Philip? Whoever has seen me has seen the Father..."

According to Jesus, seeing him is the same as seeing the Father. Seeing Jesus is the same as seeing God.

JOHN 5 & 10

We also find these encounters in John's Gospel, which speak for themselves:

But Jesus answered them, "My Father is working until now, and I am working." This was why the Jews were seeking all the more to kill him, because not only was he breaking the Sabbath, but he was even calling God his own Father, making himself equal with God. (John 5:17-18)

My sheep hear my voice, and I know them, and they follow me. I give them eternal life, and they will never perish, and no one will snatch them out of my hand. My Father, who has given them to me, is greater than all, and no one is able to snatch them out of the Father's hand. I and the Father are one."

The Jews picked up stones again to stone him. Jesus answered them, "I have shown you many good works from the Father; for which of them are you going to stone me?" The Jews answered him, "It is not for a good work that we are going to stone you but for blasphemy, because you, being a man, make yourself God." (John 10:27-33)

JOHN ONLY?

Concerning the four Gospels, scholars agree that John was written last and Mark was written first, with Matthew and Luke written between the two. Some skeptics will often try to say that John is the only Gospel where Jesus claims to be divine. They say we only see these sorts of statements by Jesus in John because his believers decided later that he was God and added them into the story of Jesus. In other words, according to them, Jesus never claims to be God in Mark, Matthew, and Luke, but by the time John wrote his Gospel, legends and myths about Jesus had formed and were added into John's Gospel. Yet, when we look at the facts, this theory is a sinking ship.

First, John was one of Jesus' original disciples. If Jesus didn't claim to be divine, then this isn't a case of legends developing and being mixed in with truth over time; this is flat-out lying! If Jesus didn't claim to be divine, John would've known it, so when he wrote his Gospel, he was purposely being deceptive. But textual criticism and the vast amount of ancient manuscripts of the New Testament we have today[122] have shown that the original writings of the New Testament haven't been changed or corrupted over time. So, the Gospel of John we read today is true to the original Gospel written by John.

Secondly, most of Paul's letters in the New Testament were written before all four Gospels were written, and they were all written before John's Gospel, and Paul clearly states Jesus is God several times (as we saw above).

Finally, Jesus *did* claim to be God in the earlier Gospels, as we see plainly in Mark, which is considered the earliest Gospel, written only about 40 years after the actual events.

MARK 2

And when Jesus saw their faith, he said to the paralytic, "Son, your sins are forgiven." Now some of the scribes were sitting there, questioning in their hearts, "Why does this man speak like that? He is blaspheming! Who can forgive sins but God alone?" (Mark 2:5-7)

Here, again, we see Jesus being accused of blasphemy. Why? He has forgiven someone's sins. And who is the only being that can forgive sins according to the Jews? God. This same event is recorded in **Luke 5** and also as a shorter version in **Matthew 9**. Thus, through his actions, Jesus clearly claims divinity in the earlier Gospels.

Do you see the issue here? We have skeptics who live two thousandyears after Jesus in a culture totally unlike the culture Jesus lived in (and many who aren't even Jewish), looking at the Gospels of

---

[122] See Chapter 3 of this book.

Mark, Matthew, and Luke and saying, "Jesus never claimed to be God." Yet, the first century Jews, who lived at the exact time and in the exact culture of Jesus, are saying, "This guy thinks he's God!" Who's more likely to understand what's going on? In fact, modern Jews who have read the Gospels have said the same thing. Michael Bird in *How God Became Jesus* quotes Jewish scholar Jacob Neusner, who admitted in an interview that he was so disturbed when reading Jesus' words, he wanted to ask, "Who do you think you are – God?"[123]

An Old Testament prophet may declare that God has forgiven a person's sins, like the prophet Nathan said to King David in **2 Samuel 12:13**, but a prophet is only God's messenger. A true prophet of God would never claim to forgive sins on his own authority. So, Jesus is either a blasphemer and a false prophet or God in the flesh. How could we possibly know for sure? Well, a miracle would be helpful:

And when Jesus saw their faith, he said to the paralytic, "Son, your sins are forgiven." Now some of the scribes were sitting there, questioning in their hearts, "Why does this man speak like that? He is blaspheming! Who can forgive sins but God alone?" And immediately Jesus, perceiving in his spirit that they thus questioned within themselves, said to them, "Why do you question these things in your hearts? Which is easier, to say to the paralytic, 'Your sins are forgiven,' or to say, 'Rise, take up your bed and walk'? But that you may know that the Son of Man has authority on earth to forgive sins" — he said to the paralytic — "I say to you, rise, pick up your bed, and go home." And he rose and immediately picked up his bed and went out before them all, so that they were all amazed and glorified God, saying, "We never saw anything like this!" (Mark 2:5-12)

---

[123] *How God Became Jesus* by Michael Bird, Craig Evans, Simon Gathercole, Charles Hill, and Chris Tilling. See Chapter 3: "Did Jesus Think He Was God?" by Michael Bird (Zondervan, 2014).

Who Jesus Ain't

MARK 14

But he remained silent and made no answer. Again the high priest asked him, "Are you the Christ, the Son of the Blessed?" And Jesus said, "I am, and you will see the Son of Man seated at the right hand of Power, and coming with the clouds of heaven." And the high priest tore his garments and said, "What further witnesses do we need? You have heard his blasphemy. What is your decision?" And they all condemned him as deserving death. (Mark 14:61-64)

Jesus makes a very lofty claim here, one that is such blasphemy that the high priest tears his clothes and they all condemn Jesus to death. Did Jesus claim to be divine? The high priest — who should know what he's talking about — certainly thought so. Sure, we could say the high priest was looking for *any* reason to get rid of Jesus, but even bloated accusations need some basis in reality.

First, Jesus affirms that he is the Son of God, the "Son of the Blessed," making himself equal with God. As we saw above in **John 5:17-18**, the Jews understood Jesus calling God "Father" (something that may not seem shocking to us today since most Christians refer to God as such) as "making himself equal with God."

There are other times the expression "Son of God" is used in the Bible when not referring to a divine being equal (or as one) with God, such as the Messiah (who was not originally thought to be divine), the Old Testament nation of Israel, and even angels. But the way Jesus claims he's God's Son, the intimacy he claims to have with God, along with the other things he's claiming (and doing), makes for a cumulating case that he's saying a lot more than just he's the Messiah or even an angel – which would be sensational claims on their own!

Take a moment and try to think like a first century Jew: Jews in Jesus' day, unlike the pagan Romans, understood that there was only one God, and everything else is *not* God. Thus, there is God, and there is everything he created. There is no third category. Therefore, when Jesus says he's the Son of God, the Jews don't understand it as Romans and think, "Ok, this guy thinks he's *part* God" or "This guy thinks he's a demi-god," they understand it correctly as Jesus saying, "I *am* God." That's why they accuse him of blasphemy, a crime worthy of death. To a Jew, something can't be *part* God. Something is either fully God or fully something else.

Secondly, in Mark 14, Jesus also calls himself the Son of Man, who will be *"seated at the right hand of Power, and coming with the clouds of heaven."* This is a reference to **Psalm 110** and **Daniel 7:13-14.**

Psalm 110 can be best summed up with its own opening lines:

The LORD says to my Lord:
"Sit at my right hand,
until I make your enemies your footstool." (Psalm 110:1)

Psalm 110, written by King David under the inspiration of the Holy Spirit, shows God, the LORD ("Yahweh," the name of God given to Moses), sitting another Lord at his right hand, a unique place of power, prestige, and honor.

"Son of Man" is Jesus' favorite way of referring to himself, which is a reference to the Book of Daniel. **Daniel 7:13-14** speaks of *"one like a son of man"* who is able to come into the presence of God ("the Ancient of Days"), which usually means death due to God's holiness and man's sin, but instead God gives him everlasting dominion and glory:

I saw in the night visions,
and behold, with the clouds of heaven
there came one like a son of man,
and he came to the Ancient of Days
and was presented before him.

Who Jesus Ain't

And to him was given dominion
  and glory and a kingdom,
that all peoples, nations, and languages
  should serve him;
his dominion is an everlasting dominion,
  which shall not pass away,
and his kingdom one
  that shall not be destroyed. (Daniel 7:13-14)

God will give to the Son of Man, because only he is worthy, a kingdom that will never end made of people from all parts of the earth.[124] Michael Bird writes that we have no evidence of anyone else in the first century (or any other century) claiming to be the Son of Man, and

> "Jesus' claim is not that he's going to sit on his own
> little throne next to God; rather, he will sit at God's
> right hand on God's throne. If Jesus thinks that Dan.
> 7:13-14 is about him, then he is placing himself
> within the orbit of divine sovereignty and claiming a
> place within the divine regency of God Almighty. If
> he's wrong, it isn't just bad theology; it is blasphemy
> and an affront to Jewish monotheism."[125]

God doesn't share his throne with anyone.

Finally, did you catch what Jesus first said in response to the high priest? He said, "I AM"! As we looked at earlier in this chapter, I AM ("Yahweh") is the exclusive name of God.

---

[124] Jesus took up this status described in Psalm 110 and Daniel 7:13-14 after his victory on the cross over sin and death, after his resurrection and ascension.
[125] *How God Became Jesus*, Chapter 3: "Did Jesus Think He Was God?" by Michael Bird.

Who Jesus Ain't

Here is **Mark 14:61-64** again:

But he remained silent and made no answer. Again the high priest asked him, "Are you the Christ, the Son of the Blessed?" And Jesus said, "I am, and you will see the Son of Man seated at the right hand of Power, and coming with the clouds of heaven." And the high priest tore his garments and said, "What further witnesses do we need? You have heard his blasphemy. What is your decision?" And they all condemned him as deserving death.

One of these three claims ("Son of God," "Son of Man," "I AM") on its own may not have raised many eyebrows. In a different context, they may have been overlooked. But as I said above, the culminating case of all of these statements along with Jesus' other words and actions is just too much for the high priest to bear. The significance of these short statements by Jesus may be lost on someone living today, but the high priest picked up on what Jesus was saying quite clearly.

According to What Authority?

Jesus demonstrates he believes he's God by speaking as with divine authority – making himself equal with God. In other words, he's saying things only God has the power and authority to declare. When he speaks, he assumes his words hold the same weight as when God speaks. We already looked at an episode where Jesus forgave someone's sins in **Mark 2:5-12**, something only God can do. Another example is when Jesus says he has authority over God's established Sabbath:

And he said to them, "The Sabbath was made for man, not man for the Sabbath. So the Son of Man is lord even of the Sabbath." (Mark 2:27-28)

Who Jesus Ain't

Obviously, if Jesus believes he can speak with God's authority, his actions illustrate this also. Thus, he breaks the Sabbath (in the eyes of the Jewish religious leaders anyway.)[126]

Additionally, when Jesus drives the money-changers and vendors out of the Temple in Jerusalem,[127] even flipping over their tables, he quotes from **Isaiah 56:7**, *"for my house shall be called a house of prayer."* Notice what he calls God's Temple: "my house." And who is speaking in Isaiah 56:7? God.

We also see this assumption of divine authority when Jesus reconfigures many of God's commandments with "But I say to you" commands:

"You have heard that it was said to those of old, 'You shall not murder; and whoever murders will be liable to judgment.' But I say to you that everyone who is angry with his brother will be liable to judgment; whoever insults his brother will be liable to the council; and whoever says, 'You fool!' will be liable to the hell of fire. (Matthew 5:21-22)

"You have heard that it was said, 'You shall not commit adultery.' But I say to you that everyone who looks at a woman with lustful intent has already committed adultery with her in his heart. (Matthew 5:27-28)

"It was also said, 'Whoever divorces his wife, let him give her a certificate of divorce.' But I say to you that everyone who divorces his wife, except on the ground of sexual immorality, makes her commit adultery, and whoever marries a divorced woman commits adultery. (Matthew 5:31-32)

---

[126] Mark 2:23-28.

[127] Luke 19:45-46; Matthew 21:12-13; Mark 11:15-17.

"You have heard that it was said, 'An eye for an eye and a tooth for a tooth.' But I say to you, Do not resist the one who is evil. But if anyone slaps you on the right cheek, turn to him the other also. (Matthew 5:38-39)

It should be noted that Jesus is not *changing* God's laws with his "But I say to you" commandments, but *interpreting them correctly*. Jesus said in **Matthew 5:17** that he didn't come to do away with God's law, but to fulfill it.

Both foe and friend throughout the Gospels recognize the fact that Jesus was teaching with an authority higher than a prophet, priest, or any of the religious leaders of his day:

And they came again to Jerusalem. And as he was walking in the temple, the chief priests and the scribes and the elders came to him, and they said to him, "By what authority are you doing these things, or who gave you this authority to do them?" (Mark 11:27-28)

And when Jesus finished these sayings, the crowds were astonished at his teaching, for he was teaching them as one who had authority, and not as their scribes. (Matthew 7:28-29)

No One Expected

No one expected God to become a man, and no one expected the Messiah to be God.[128] Surely, his fellow Jews would've killed Jesus

---

[128] Though a prophecy about the Messiah in Isaiah 9:6 does read:

For to us a child is born,
   to us a son is given;
and the government shall be upon his shoulder,
   and his name shall be called
Wonderful Counselor, Mighty God,

sooner if he had openly pronounced himself as God, and the Romans would've killed him sooner had he openly pronounced himself the Messiah, a king, a rival threat to the Roman Empire. Instead, we see him usually referring to himself as the Son of Man, speaking in parables to mask his message,[129] telling those who understand who he is to keep quiet about it,[130] and allowing his actions to speak for him.[131] Despite this, word about Jesus of Nazareth spread, and Jesus willingly went to his death on a cross for the sins of the world after only three years of ministry.

Sometimes skeptics (and Jehovah's Witnesses) look at Jesus' claims and invent another interpretation, such as Jesus wasn't claiming to be God but an exalted angel or a demi-god of some sort. Again, this is an example of people who live thousands of years after the events looking back at an unfamiliar culture and inserting their own ideas into Jesus' story. Jesus was a first century Jew living among other first century Jews, and they understood the context of what he was saying. As D.A. Carson says in his book *Jesus the Son of God*,[132] Jesus "is not just David's heir and thus the Son of God by virtue of being the Davidic king [the Messiah], but he is also the Son of God by virtue of his preexistence and unqualified divine status. No angel can match him on either score."

No, Jesus never came out and stated blatantly, "Hey, everyone, I'm God!" So what? I can claim I'm God. Would you believe me? Jesus understood actions speak louder than words. The miracles Jesus performed weren't simply entertaining tricks to impress his audience. Each miracle was showing to his audience who he truly is. In the Old

---

Everlasting Father, Prince of Peace.

[129] See Mark 4.
[130] See Mark 7:36 & 8:30 and Luke 4:41.
[131] See John 10:25 & 10:37-38.
[132] *Jesus the Son of God: A Christological Title Often Overlooked, Sometimes Misunderstood, and Currently Disputed* by D.A. Carson (Crossway, 2012).

Testament, God fed the Israelites in the wilderness with manna from Heaven; Jesus fed the 5,000 with five loaves of bread and two fish. God parted the Red Sea for Israel to escape death at the hands of the Egyptians; Jesus walked on the sea and calmed the storm. God turned the Nile into blood; Jesus turned water into wine. In fact, John in his Gospel doesn't use the word "miracle" to describe Jesus' miraculous actions. He calls them "signs." They're signs of who Jesus is. *"The blind receive their sight, the lame walk, lepers are cleansed, and the deaf hear, the dead are raised up, the poor have good news preached to them"*[133] – all signs that God's Kingdom has come. All are signs that God is renewing his fallen creation.

When Jesus calms a raging sea, the disciples ask, *"What sort of man is this, that even winds and sea obey him?"*[134] Matthew doesn't give us the answer because he wants us to figure it out, just as the disciples did. As we saw earlier, Jesus gives us the answer in **John 14:9**, *"Whoever has seen me has seen the Father."* Jesus of Nazareth, God the Son, the Son of God, the Son of Man, is *"the radiance of God's glory and the exact representation of his being."*[135]

Further, Jesus rose from the dead after being executed on a Roman cross; this is the ultimate evidence that Jesus is who he said he is. Not only did Jesus predict his death and resurrection,[136] but he also claimed that he had the authority to do so:

For this reason the Father loves me, because I lay down my life that I may take it up again. No one takes it from me, but I lay it down of my own accord. I have authority to lay it down, and I have authority to take it up again. (John 10:17-18)

---

[133] Luke 7:22; Matthew 11:5.
[134] Matthew 8:27.
[135] Hebrews 1:3.
[136] See John 2:18-22; Matthew 12:39-40, 16:21, 27:62-64.

Who Jesus Ain't

Again, first century Jews knew only God had authority over life and death.

Would God Raise a Blasphemer from the Dead?

Many people say things like, "I believe Jesus was a good man, but I don't believe he was God" or "I believe Jesus was wise, and I live by his teachings, but I don't believe the supernatural stuff." The thing is, you can't believe Jesus is wise or good if you don't believe he's God. In other words, you can't believe Jesus is wise or good if you believe he really said everything he said. Let me explain:

C.S. Lewis, the famous writer of *The Lion, the Witch, and the Wardrobe* (and also an Oxford professor and former atheist) made popular what is sometimes called the "Lunatic, Liar, or Lord" argument. Basically, the argument goes like this: Jesus claimed to be God, so if he's not telling the truth, then he's a liar. If he's a liar, he can't be good. Further, if Jesus *really* believed he was God, but he *wasn't*, then he's not a liar (because he believes it's true) but he's crazy; he's a lunatic. If he's a lunatic, he's not wise. Okay, I suppose there can be wise (and even good) lunatics out there, but I wouldn't trust my life to one! The only other option then is that Jesus is Lord, as in Lord God.

If we pick-and-choose what we want to believe Jesus said, then we're not really following Jesus, are we? We're following ourselves and making Jesus into someone he's not. But if we choose to follow everything Jesus said, then we have to believe he was more – much more – than just a wise or good man: he was God in the flesh.

Not only this, but we have to ask ourselves a question: Would God raise a blasphemer from the grave? As we've seen, Jesus claimed to be God in the flesh. If he were not, then he was either a liar or a lunatic. And not only would he *not* be God, but he would be directly opposing God; he would be a heretic and blasphemer, someone disgracing God's name and the wrath of God would be on him. Yet, Jesus rose from the dead, something no man can do. If Jesus were lying about being God, would God endorse him by raising him from the dead? I think not. In fact, there have been many liars and lunatics in history who claimed to be God, and once they were dead they stayed dead.

CHAPTER 10:
JESUS AIN'T
A MYTH OR LEGEND
PART 2

TRUE STORY, BRO.

There was once this guy. He was a really nice guy, and he helped a lot of people with his amazing powers. He could even control the weather. One time, this nice guy brought someone back from the dead. In fact, if you think that's impressive, he was killed and placed in a tomb, but he was resurrected. He was the one and only son of his father, who sent him to Earth as a child. And this guy's name is...

Who Jesus Ain't

Superman.

In this chapter, I will be arguing that the creators of Superman blatantly borrowed from the life of Jesus of Nazareth as recorded in the New Testament.

After all, Jesus was a really nice guy who helped a lot of people with his amazing powers. In **Mark 4:35-41**, Jesus controls the weather by calming a storm while on a boat. He also brought Lazarus back from the dead in **John 11**. Furthermore, he was killed and placed in a tomb, and he was resurrected. He was the one and only Son of God the Father, who sent his eternal Son to Earth to be born as a child through Mary.

OK, Seriously

Actually, I have no intentions of arguing here that Superman is just a rip-off of Jesus, but if you had read my arguments as I presented them above, and you didn't know any better, and you let the discussion end there, you probably would have been convinced. Or you may be the suspicious type. You may know a little something about both Jesus and Superman and raise some objections:

Wait, Superman couldn't control the weather! When did Superman bring anyone back from the dead? In fact, when did Superman die and resurrect?

And this would be where my arguments start to fall apart:
ME: *Superman at times would use his super breath and blow really hard and it produced powerful wind. And at the end of the first Superman movie, the 1978 version with Christopher Reeve, when Lois Lane dies, Superman flies around the earth so fast in the opposite direction of the earth's spin that he changes the direction of Earth's rotation and literally*

rewinds time so he is able to rescue Lois Lane before she dies.[137] *Then, in the early 1990's, DC Comics ran the storyline "The Death of Superman" where Superman was killed in a battle with Doomsday, but Superman returned after a long hiatus.*

YOU: *Having super breath isn't anything like controlling the weather. Rewinding time by flying around the earth to save someone before they die – though incredible*[138] *– is not the same as bringing someone back from the dead. And maybe Superman sort of "died" for a time and returned, but he was restored in a "regeneration matrix" in the Fortress of Solitude. Anyhow, if there's anywhere where people are killed and brought back to life, it's in comic books! It happens all the time! None of this is anything like Jesus' life.*

ME: *But what about the other stuff I said?*

YOU: *Superman was from the planet Krypton and his father was Jor-El. Jesus was the incarnation of the eternal Son of God of the Trinitarian God. Jesus and Superman were both usually nice guys and do help people with their powers, but Jesus performed miracles because he was divine. For instance, he healed the sick and the lame. Superman had powers because he was an alien from space. Jesus didn't perform feats of incredible strength like Superman. Or fly. Or shoot lasers from his eyes.*

ME: *They were both their fathers' one and only son.*

YOU: *OK, I guess I'll give you that one.*

ME: *Also, the regeneration matrix in the Fortress of Solitude was like the tomb Jesus was placed in and emerged resurrected from.*

---

[137] Thankfully, for all our sakes, Superman corrected the spin of the earth again. Even when watching this as a young boy, I thought this ending was ridiculous and spoiled what was an otherwise cool movie.

[138] Corny, actually.

Who Jesus Ain't

YOU: *Now you're getting carried away again.*

Do you find the above argument about Superman and Jesus ridiculous? Sadly, this is hardly any different than serious arguments about Jesus being a copycat of any number of pagan myths.

Whenever someone tries to argue that there are similarities between Christianity and pagan mystery religions – sometimes called the "Pagan Copycat Theory" or what I like to call the "Pagan Myth Myth" (no, I'm not stuttering) – the arguments often go like the one above about Superman and Jesus. Or they *should* go like that anyway. Thus, we need to know how to reply to those who make these claims (and it's fairly easy).

The copycat theory, the idea that Christianity is simply a Frankenstein-like cut-and-paste religion made from long dead pagan mystery religions is the actual dead thing here. The debate has long been over in scholarly circles because the "evidence" was weak from the start, and solid evidence clearly points to what we all knew from the beginning: Christianity started in the ancient Jewish land of Judea, spread by the Jewish followers of the Jewish Jesus of Nazareth.

The copycat theory is an old theory that has long been refuted, and no new evidence to support it has arisen. Yet, the "Misinformation Age" of modern media keeps the pagan copycat accusations coming back every Easter and Christmas holiday season like that bad mayo on that club sandwich you keep burping up and tasting.

Thanks for the continued life of these copycat theories can be given to the Internet and to conspiracy videos like *Zeitgeist*. As Mark W. Foreman writes in his essay "Challenging the Zeitgeist Movie:

Parallelomania on Steroids" in the book *Come Let Us Reason*,[139] "Arguments don't stop being bad simply because of their upgraded, flashy attire."

Here are the issues with these copycat theories:

1. A Bad Start

To begin with, many making these claims are starting off with a poor understanding of the specific pagan mystery religions they're citing anyway. These pagan religions are called "mystery religions" simply because, well… they're mysteries.

Pagan mystery religions held to secret teachings that only those indoctrinated into the religion knew. The followers of these religions took vows of secrecy. Thus, there's not a lot of material out there about their specific beliefs and practices.

Unlike Christianity, the mystery religions didn't have books – scriptures or any records – that explained their beliefs. Moreover, because of this, there was a lot of diversity. For most, not one authoritative story on which the religion is based exists. Knowledge of these religions come from scattered sources, such as inscriptions or art. For instance, all we know about Mithraism, a late Roman mystery religion, comes from graffiti, statues, and some writings from Christian and neo-Platonist outsiders.

So, it's sort of like putting together a puzzle, but we can't use the shape of the pieces to guide us on how they fit together. For example, Mark

---

[139] *Come Let Us Reason*, edited by Paul Copan and William Lane Craig (B & H Publishing Group, 2012). See Chapter 10:"Does the Story of Jesus Mimic Pagan Mystery Stories" by Mary Jo Sharp and Chapter 11: "Challenging the Zeitgeist Movie: Parallelomania on Steroids" by Mark W. Foreman.

W. Foreman points out that the conspiracy documentary *Zeitgeist* does this with Horus, the Egyptian god. The *Zeitgeist* version of Horus is "pieced together from a number of sources, some of which conflict."

Thus, some of those proposing a connection between Christianity and pagan religions often not only have a poor understanding of Christianity, but also are basing their understanding of pagan religions on what are probably not even accurate portrayals of the pagan mystery religions to begin with.

2. Exaggerations & Blatant Fabrications

This is the biggest issue with these copycat theories. As with the Superman argument above, many of the supposed parallels between Christianity and paganism are unabashed exaggerations (which call for large leaps in logic) or downright lies.

(To be fair, some people passing along these theories – perhaps on Facebook or a blog – may not be aware they're passing along lies, but some of these claims are so outrageous someone *had* to know they were being dishonest in starting them.)

For instance, it has been claimed that Krishna was born to a virgin. Krishna, a Hindu god, was the eighth son of his mother! That's a pretty loose definition of "virgin"! My favorite claim is the one that says the Roman god Mithras was born of a virgin. How this idea ever came about is befuddling because Mithras was born from a rock! (But I guess rocks can be considered virgins, right?)

Let's think of it this way: Was Jesus a copy of Horus... or Mithras... or Dionysus...or Krishna... or Attis... or Asclepius? People have tried to argue that Jesus is a rip off of every one of these gods. Even if it's possible that he was a copycat of *one* of them, it's implausible that he was a copycat of *all* of them, which means even if one theory is right, the vast majority of them are wrong.

One strategy used to mislead is to use Christian terminology to describe events or details in pagan myths to make them sound much more Christian than they actually are. Above, I describe Superman's emergence out of the regeneration matrix in the Fortress of Solitude after his sort-of death as him being "resurrected." I even attempt to call the regeneration matrix "a tomb" to illustrate this point, and though it may seem like a stretch, it's no more of a stretch than the actual claims of some of these copycat theorists.

For instance, there have been claims that Krishna and Attis, a Greek god, were "crucified." Actually, Krishna was shot in the foot with an arrow. Attis castrated himself and died! I have a feeling neither case is quite what would come to mind for the Romans when they heard the word "crucified." Likewise, D. M. Murdock in his book *Christ in Egypt: The Jesus-Horus Connection* claims that artistic depictions of Egyptian gods, including Horus, show many of them crucified. Yet, what he means is simply that these gods had their arms extended or outstretched![140] Does that mean every time someone yawns and stretches out their arms, they're being crucified?

Further, just like my Superman argument above, proponents of the Christian/pagan myth theory like to cherry-pick information to "expose" supposed parallels. Yet, when the Christian and pagan accounts are read as a whole and compared, the similarities are hardly similarities at all.

For example, claims have been made that dying and resurrected gods were a regular theme in pagan myths. Often Osiris, an Egyptian god, is one of the prime examples. Yet, Osiris didn't return to life in the world

---

[140] See *Come Let Us Reason*, Chapter 11:"Challenging the Zeitgeist Movie: Parallelomania on Steroids" by Mark W. Foreman.

of the living; he became the king of the netherworld – the underworld, the land of the dead. The only dying and rising gods found have all been related to the continuous, never-ending life-and-death cycle of vegetation and the seasons. These are hardly comparable to the death by crucifixion and the one-time resurrection of Jesus three days later.

Christian apologist William Lane Craig tells of a time he once debated Robert Price on Jesus' resurrection. Price claimed that Jesus' healing miracles were copied from the healing stories of Asclepius, the Greek god of medicine and healing. So, Craig insisted Price read to the audience from his primary source about Asclepius. Once Price read the primary source, the lack of similarities became obvious to all.[141] This is an "overemphasis on (supposed) similarities between two things while ignoring the vast and relevant differences between them," Mark W. Foreman writes.

The only similarity I've come across that may be legitimate is with the Greek god Dionysus – called Bacchus in Roman mythology. Dionysus certainly turned water into wine. Jesus performed his first known public miracle in **John 2** by turning water into wine. But the similarities end there. And, let me point out, Dionysus was, after all, the god of wine – and sexual ecstasy – and he liked to party.

3. Wrong Chronology

As stated above, pagan mystery religions changed over time because they didn't have scripture that was strictly held to like Christianity. Furthermore, they were open to blending other religions and beliefs. Today, Christianity may have many denominations with different traditions or different interpretations of minor doctrines, but the core of Christianity has stayed the same for 2,000 years because we have the

---

[141] www.reasonablefaith.org/jesus-and-pagan-mythology#ixzz2yp7eGU68

Bible to always refer back to. On the other hand, there are many versions of the pagan mystery religions and their myths.

Often, when some sort of parallel is made between paganism and Christianity that looks legitimate (and not an extreme exaggeration or fabrication), it has been found the similar characteristic didn't appear in that pagan religion's history until long *after* Christianity had been established. Thus, it appears Christianity influenced the pagan religion, not the other way around.

For example, the Christian similarities with the mystery religions of Mithras, Osiris, Horus, and Attis/Adonis are all found over 100 years *after* the rise of Christianity, and claims of the Hindu god Krishna's resurrection don't appear until the 6th or 7th Century.

Mithras, whose worship was popular with Roman soldiers, is often connected to Jesus. Mithras was a Persian god dating as far back as the 14th Century BC, but in an interview with Lee Stobel in *The Case For the Real Jesus*[142], Dr. Edwin M. Yamauchi explains that Mithras didn't appear in Rome until 66 AD. But this is still "not the same" version of Mithras found in the Roman mystery religion. Moreover, most of the evidence for Mithraism comes from the 2nd, 3rd, and 4th Centuries AD. Jesus died on the cross in the 1st Century, around 33 AD. Evidence refutes the claim that Mithras was called "savior" before Jesus, because the evidence is from an inscription dated after Christianity was proclaiming Jesus as savior. In short, the Roman version of Mithraism developed after the New Testament was written.

There is "no evidence that there was any pagan mystery influence in first-century Palestine," Mark W. Foreman writes. Mystery religions reached their peak in the Mediterranean in the 2nd and 3rd Centuries, and there's little evidence of these beliefs being there in the 1st Century.

---

[142] *The Case For the Real Jesus* by Lee Strobel (Zondervan, 2007).

4. Logical Leaps & the Nature of Religion

Logically, we have to remember that even if a similarity exists between Jesus and a pagan god (and it doesn't run into the issues mentioned above), that doesn't automatically mean they are related, copied, or influenced. A connection must be proved.

Religions, by nature, will have some general things in common, like beliefs about an afterlife and supernatural forces; many religions, like Christianity, have some sort of tradition with a common meal. Similarity alone doesn't prove dependence.

5. Christianity's Nature

Finally, Christianity, like Judaism, has always been an exclusivist faith. Throughout the Bible, God's people are explicitly warned again-and-again against mixing their faith with other religions and from straying away from God's Word as it had been given to them. See Paul's letter to the Galatians, for example:

But even if we or an angel from heaven should preach to you a gospel contrary to the one we preached to you, let him be accursed. As we have said before, so now I say again: If anyone is preaching to you a gospel contrary to the one you received, let him be accursed. (Galatians 1:8-9)

Paul says if anyone teaches something different from what has been laid out by Jesus, that person should be cursed, and Paul says this includes "we" – meaning him and the other apostles – and even angels! Not even Jesus' own apostles or the angels have the authority to change Jesus' message. You don't get much more clear than that! Furthermore, Jesus,

Who Jesus Ain't

Peter, John, Paul, and Jude all warned against false teachers who corrupt the message of Jesus.[143]

Unlike Christianity, paganism emphasized feelings and experience over doctrine and belief, and the mixing of differing religious beliefs was normal practice to the pagans. What's more likely: pagan religions borrowing from Christianity or Christianity borrowing from pagans?

---

[143] See Matthew 7:15; 2 Timothy 4:3-4; 1 John 4:1; 2 Peter 2:1-3.

CHAPTER 11: JESUS AIN'T RELIGIOUS

When I read the Bible for the first time, I was pleasantly surprised at just how anti-religious Jesus was. I had been anti-religious myself for most of my life. I had begun to think religion was silly at a pretty young age, and by the time I was in college, I considered myself an atheist – or at least a strong agnostic. Though I often wavered between atheism and agnosticism, the one thing I was certain about was that religion – any and all religion – was silly. So, after the Holy Spirit opened my eyes, and I started looking into Jesus of Nazareth, I was both shocked and pleased (and even comforted) by Jesus' disdain for meaningless ritual and religious hypocrites.

Who Jesus Ain't

Before we move on, let me take a moment to be clear about what I mean by "religion." By religion, I mean rituals people do in hopes of manipulating a god or gods into blessing them. Yes, I use that word "manipulate" purposely. Because when you get down to it, that's what religion is; it's literally about doing things in hopes that you can manipulate a god, gods, or God to get what you want. Religion looks to some supernatural being like a genie in a bottle to grant wishes. Just like you have to get the right combination to open your locker in high school, religion teaches that all you have to do is get the right combination to open your divine sugar daddy's vault of favors.

Of course, if you're doing these rituals in honor of the wrong god, all you're doing is wasting your time. You might as well be praying to a chair. Or you could be following the right religion, but honoring your god in the wrong way. As an atheist/agnostic I, of course, believed there was no right religion, and so all religious rituals were pointless. Religion was just an organized form of superstition.

With this, there are also in Christian circles (and all religions) the hypocrites, people who follow Christian "ritual" but they don't follow Jesus in their daily lives. Again, their ritual is pointless. It's superstition. These hypocrites go to church and go through all of the motions – they even talk a good game – but a person's daily life is the strongest testament of their faith. No Christian is perfect, but I'm speaking of those who proclaim to be Christian but live in clear contradiction to the teachings of Scripture.

If the above description is how we choose to define "religion," then I don't consider true, biblical Christianity a religion. Of course, religion can be simply defined as a belief in a divine being or beings. If that's the definition, then Christianity is certainly a religion. But true, biblical Christianity is not about rituals or superstition, but a God-man. And this God-man railed against empty rituals, false religion, and the hypocritically self-righteous. This God-man embodied true religion –

the one and only true religion. Outside of Jesus of Nazareth, everything else is superstition.

We'll talk more about this below, but first let's just enjoy Jesus ripping into some religious hypocrites:

And in his teaching he said, "Beware of the scribes, who like to walk around in long robes and like greetings in the marketplaces and have the best seats in the synagogues and the places of honor at feasts, who devour widows' houses and for a pretense make long prayers. They will receive the greater condemnation." (Mark 12:38-40)

And as Jesus reclined at table in the house, behold, many tax collectors and sinners came and were reclining with Jesus and his disciples. And when the Pharisees saw this, they said to his disciples, "Why does your teacher eat with tax collectors and sinners?" But when he heard it, he said, "Those who are well have no need of a physician, but those who are sick. Go and learn what this means, 'I desire mercy, and not sacrifice.'[144] *For I came not to call the righteous, but sinners." (Matthew 9:10-13)*

In **Matthew 15**, when the Pharisees and scribes ask Jesus, *"Why do your disciples break the tradition of the elders? For they do not wash their hands when they eat."* Jesus simply shoots back, *"And why do you break the commandment of God for the sake of your tradition?"*[145] and he quotes **Isaiah 29:13** to them,

"'This people honors me [God] with their lips,
but their heart is far from me;
in vain do they worship me,
teaching as doctrines the commandments of men.'"

---

[144] From Hosea 6:6.
[145] Matthew 15:2-3.

Ouch. He also calls them *"blind guides. And if the blind lead the blind, both will fall into a pit."*[146] Double ouch.

Chapter 23 of Matthew is the mother of all beat-downs of religious hypocrites. I recommend reading the whole chapter, but here are some highlights:

Then Jesus said to the crowds and to his disciples, "The scribes and the Pharisees sit on Moses' seat, so do and observe whatever they tell you, but not the works they do. For they preach, but do not practice. They tie up heavy burdens, hard to bear, and lay them on people's shoulders, but they themselves are not willing to move them with their finger. (Matthew 23:1-4)

Woe to you, scribes and Pharisees, hypocrites! For you tithe mint and dill and cumin, and have neglected the weightier matters of the law: justice and mercy and faithfulness. These you ought to have done, without neglecting the others. You blind guides, straining out a gnat and swallowing a camel! (Matthew 23:23-24)

Woe to you, scribes and Pharisees, hypocrites! For you clean the outside of the cup and the plate, but inside they are full of greed and self-indulgence. You blind Pharisee! First clean the inside of the cup and the plate, that the outside also may be clean.

Woe to you, scribes and Pharisees, hypocrites! For you are like whitewashed tombs, which outwardly appear beautiful, but within are full of dead people's bones and all uncleanness. So you also outwardly appear righteous to others, but within you are full of hypocrisy and lawlessness. (Matthew 23:25-28)

In Jesus' famous Sermon on the Mount, he addresses the empty rituals and empty "good works" hypocrites do to look righteous, hoping to

---

[146] Matthew 15:14.

gain praise for themselves from man rather than honoring God with their actions:

Beware of practicing your righteousness before other people in order to be seen by them, for then you will have no reward from your Father who is in heaven.

Thus, when you give to the needy, sound no trumpet before you, as the hypocrites do in the synagogues and in the streets, that they may be praised by others. Truly, I say to you, they have received their reward. (Matthew 6:1-2)

And when you pray, you must not be like the hypocrites. For they love to stand and pray in the synagogues and at the street corners, that they may be seen by others. Truly, I say to you, they have received their reward. (Matthew 6:5)

What Jesus means is that the religious hypocrites have received their reward already in their earthly status and in the earthly praise they lust for, but that's the extent of their reward. They'll receive nothing from God except "the greater condemnation."[147]

OK, let's look at one example from the Gospel of John:

Jesus said to them, "If God were your Father, you would love me, for I came from God and I am here. I came not of my own accord, but he sent me. Why do you not understand what I say? It is because you cannot bear to hear my word. You are of your father the devil, and your will is to do your father's desires. He was a murderer from the beginning, and does not stand in the truth, because there is no truth in him. When he lies, he speaks out of his own character, for he is a liar and the father of lies. But because I tell the truth, you do not believe me. Which one of you convicts me of sin? If I tell the truth, why do you

---

[147] Mark 12:40.

not believe me? Whoever is of God hears the words of God. The reason why you do not hear them is that you are not of God." (John 8:42-47)

Additionally, Jesus (and almost every writer of the New Testament) warns against false religious teachers and prophets:

Beware of false prophets, who come to you in sheep's clothing but inwardly are ravenous wolves. You will recognize them by their fruits. Are grapes gathered from thornbushes, or figs from thistles? So, every healthy tree bears good fruit, but the diseased tree bears bad fruit. A healthy tree cannot bear bad fruit, nor can a diseased tree bear good fruit. Every tree that does not bear good fruit is cut down and thrown into the fire. Thus you will recognize them by their fruits. (Matthew 7:15-20)

Something I recognized right away during my first time reading through the Gospels was that Jesus is patient with most sinners, but not so with the religious hypocrites. It's as if he's saying, *Everyone has sin and falls short of the glory of God – but you religious leaders, you should know better!*

The Easiest & the Hardest Religion

Humans are religious creatures. Made in God's image, we are created to know and glorify God. But since we're fallen and we love our sin more than God, we worship everything but the only thing that's worthy of worship. This may mean anything from worshipping counterfeit gods by following a false religion or our own invented "spirituality" to worshipping material things or even ourselves.

Romans 1:18-25 is sobering:

For the wrath of God is revealed from heaven against all ungodliness and unrighteousness of men, who by their unrighteousness suppress the truth. For what can be known about God is plain to them, because God has shown it to them. For his invisible attributes, namely, his eternal power and divine nature, have been clearly perceived, ever since the creation of the world, in the things that have been made. So they are without excuse. For although they knew God, they did not honor him as God or give thanks to him, but they became futile in their thinking, and their foolish hearts were darkened. Claiming to be wise, they became fools, and exchanged the glory of the immortal God for images resembling mortal man and birds and animals and creeping things.

Therefore God gave them up in the lusts of their hearts to impurity, to the dishonoring of their bodies among themselves, because they exchanged the truth about God for a lie and worshiped and served the creature rather than the Creator, who is blessed forever! Amen.

Because of our love of sin, we worship everything but the one we were created to glorify. We worship the good things God has blessed us with in his Creation, but not the Creator. Because of our stubborn opposition to God, even when faced with the true religion of Jesus of Nazareth, we still corrupt it. We try to make it something it's not. Instead of turning to the Son of God, we turn to superstition. We try to make it all about rituals. For example, how many people who call themselves Christians think they're "going to Heaven" because they attend church regularly? Yes, belonging to a church is important for a Christian, but if someone thinks this wins him salvation, then he has turned Christianity into a religion about manipulating God. The person isn't going to church to learn about God and to grow in his likeness, but to attempt to put God in his debt, to make God owe him salvation. It's much easier to have a checklist of ritual "to do's" than to truly follow Jesus with all of your life.

Jesus' words in **Matthew 7:21-23** should cause us some sober self-reflection:

Who Jesus Ain't

"Not everyone who says to me, 'Lord, Lord,' will enter the kingdom of heaven, but the one who does the will of my Father who is in heaven. On that day many will say to me, 'Lord, Lord, did we not prophesy in your name, and cast out demons in your name, and do many mighty works in your name?' And then will I declare to them, 'I never knew you; depart from me, you workers of lawlessness.'

No, calling yourself a Christian doesn't give you salvation. Being born into a Christian family doesn't give you salvation, nor does simply going to church or participating in Christian "rituals." Being a "good" person doesn't win you salvation either.

In fact, salvation is nothing that we can earn. Quite the opposite of the idea that being "good" will get you into Heaven, the overall story of the Bible tells us we all have sin and fall short of the glory of God,[148] and because we love our sin, we condemn ourselves,[149] storing up God's wrath against us.[150] The New Testament even tells us because of sin, we're God's enemies,[151] and the result of sin is death[152] — both physically and spiritually.

Think of it this way, if God is perfectly good and holy, any amount of sin – no matter how small we think it is – separates us from him. And if you don't think this is the way it should be, you don't have a high enough view of God or a low enough view of sin. Since God is perfectly good and holy, he simply *can't* overlook sin.

This may sound odd, saying God *can't* do something. God is omnipotent and the creator of all things, so can't he do everything? Not so. There are things God can't do. God can't do what's logically

---

[148] Romans 3:23, 5:12.

[149] Romans 2:1.

[150] Romans 2:5.

[151] Romans 5:10.

[152] Romans 6:23.

impossible; he can't make a square circle or a married bachelor. God also can't do things contrary to his own divine nature, which includes his perfect goodness. Thus, God can't do evil, such as lie,[153] or tempt others to do evil.[154] Likewise, God can't simply let sin go unpunished or else he wouldn't be perfectly good and holy.

But now we have a problem, a big problem. God created us to know him, and God loves us, but we're also deserving of his wrath. So, what can we do? Nothing. What can God do? Actually, there was only *one thing* he could do: he became a man named Jesus of Nazareth, lived the sinless life none of us can, and then he died a death he didn't deserve. Since he is man, he can represent us. Since he is God, his perfect sacrifice can cover us all.

And now, the work is done. It's complete. It's finished. Nothing can be added to it or improved upon. There's nothing more to do, and there's nothing we can do to earn it or deserve it. There's no manipulating God or making a deal with him. All we can do is believe God did this for us, repent of our sins (which means a changing of our minds – a turning from the world to pursue Jesus), and embrace this free gift.

Romans 6:23 tells us the bad news about our sin, but look at what else it tells us:

For the wages of sin is death, but the free gift of God is eternal life in Christ Jesus our Lord.

Ephesians 2:3-10 lays it out clearly:

...we all once lived in the passions of our flesh, carrying out the desires of the body and the mind, and were by nature children of wrath, like the rest of mankind. But God, being rich in mercy, because of the great

---

[153] Numbers 23:19; Titus 1:2; Hebrews 6:18.
[154] James 1:13.

*love with which he loved us, even when we were dead in our trespasses,
made us alive together with Christ – by grace you have been saved –
and raised us up with him and seated us with him in the heavenly
places in Christ Jesus, so that in the coming ages he might show the
immeasurable riches of his grace in kindness toward us in Christ Jesus.
(Ephesians 2:3-7)*

As if that doesn't state it clearly enough, the apostle Paul continues,
wanting to be absolutely certain we know that we're saved from
spiritual death by God's mercy alone:

*For by grace you have been saved through faith. And this is not your
own doing; it is the gift of God, not a result of works, so that no one
may boast. (Ephesians 2:8-9)*

We are saved by grace alone.[155] Salvation is a free gift.[156] And like all
gifts, we can accept it or reject it. But the one thing we definitely can't
do is earn it. Take careful note of Paul's next sentence in Ephesians:

*For we are his workmanship, created in Christ Jesus for good works,
which God prepared beforehand, that we should walk in them.
(Ephesians 2:10)*

So, we don't earn God's salvation. We don't even deserve it. And we
can't manipulate God to get it. So, why be a good person then? Because
we're created in God's image, and God is love,[157] and we love because
God first loved us.[158]

---

[155] Also see Romans 11:6: "But if it is by grace, it is no longer on the basis of
works; otherwise grace would no longer be grace."

[156] Romans 5:15-16.

[157] 1 John 4:8.

[158] 1 John 4:19.

Who Jesus Ain't

You see, Jesus turned religion on its head. Religion says be a "good" person, do these rituals, do X, Y, and Z, and then you'll earn your salvation. The Christian faith, as revealed through Jesus of Nazareth, says the opposite: You can't earn salvation, but God has earned it for you. And once you understand and accept this free gift, you obey and love God and love others not because you feel you have to, but because you want to. You want to love because God loved you first. In fact, he loved you so much that he was tortured and experienced death so you can spend eternity with him. That's love. Love motivates much more than fear or guilt or shame or obligation. And love motivates love. Good works don't lead to salvation; good works are the result of salvation.

I once had a friendly conversation with a Muslim about our faiths. As we talked, we both noticed many similarities. (Let it be noted that Muhammad, the founder of Islam, lived about 600 years after Jesus.) But as we neared the end of our conversation, I really wanted him to understand the Gospel - the good news - of Jesus. So, I explained that salvation is through Jesus's death alone and we can't earn salvation - it's a free gift from God given to us by God's grace alone - and once we understand this and are given this salvation, we want to do good works, love others, and live to honor God out of love for what he did for us. Do you know how my Muslim friend responded? Taken aback a little, he said, "That's the exact opposite of what we believe."

If you read the New Testament, you'll find a noticeable lack of ritual in Christianity. Baptism is a symbolic act done only once by a Christian to declare his or her new life in Jesus. Communion, the Lord's Supper, is done in remembrance of Jesus' sacrifice on the cross.[159] And, yes, it's essential that Christians belong to a church, read the Bible, and pray, but the purposes of these acts aren't to earn salvation or to win God's favor. If someone declares Jesus as their Lord and Savior, salvation is

---

[159] Luke 22:19-20.

already given to them. Then, motivated by love, he or she tries to live according to Jesus' perfect model.

Jesus said,

Come to me, all who labor and are heavy laden, and I will give you rest. Take my yoke upon you, and learn from me, for I am gentle and lowly in heart, and you will find rest for your souls. For my yoke is easy, and my burden is light." (Matthew 11:2-30)

But he also said,

"If anyone should come after me, let him deny himself and take up his cross daily and follow me. For whoever would save his life will lose it, but whoever loses his life for my sake will save it. For what does it profit a man if he gains the whole world and loses or forfeits himself? For whoever is ashamed of me and of my words, of him will the Son of Man be ashamed when he comes in his glory and the glory of the Father and of the holy angels. (Luke 9:23-26)

And as if that isn't intimidating enough, Jesus also said, *"If the world hates you, know that it has hated me before it hated you"*[160] and *"you will be hated by all for my name's sake."*[161]

Following Jesus is not about rituals or superstition; it's about allowing Jesus to permeate into every aspect of your life. Biblical Christianity isn't about earning salvation; it's about living out the reality of your salvation in every step of your daily walk. Christianity is the easiest religion, but it's also the hardest.

---

[160] John 15:18.
[161] Matthew 10:22.

Who Jesus Ain't

Biblical Christianity is the exact opposite of all other religions. Jesus of Nazareth has shown us this one true religion. In fact, he modeled it for us, and we're to follow him.

The apostle John tells us, *"Whoever says 'I know him' but does not keep his commandments is a liar, and the truth is not in him, but whoever keeps his word, in him truly the love of God is perfected. By this we may know that we are in him: whoever says he abides in him ought to walk in the same way in which he walked." (1 John 2:4-6)*

Jesus himself, after doing the lowly work of a servant by washing his disciples' feet, said,

For I have given you an example, that you also should do just as I have done to you... By this all people will know that you are my disciples, if you have love for one another. (John 13:15 & 13:35)

And, as if to make himself clear beyond a shadow of doubt, Jesus also said,

"If anyone loves me, he will keep my word, and my Father will love him, and we will come to him and make our home with him. Whoever does not love me does not keep my words." (John 14:23-24)

CHAPTER 12:
JESUS AIN'T
A PLURALIST OR
UNIVERSALIST

Put simply, a pluralist or Universalist is a person who believes there is more than one way to God and salvation. Thus, religions such as Christianity, Judaism, and Islam are wrong in claiming that they hold the one exclusive path to knowing God and having salvation from punishment due to sin. So, was Jesus a pluralist or Universalist? All we have to do is read **John 4** to find the answer.

In **John 4**, Jesus and his disciples are passing through Samaria, which sits between Galilee and Judea, and Jesus is left alone at Jacob's Well as his disciples go into the city to buy food. A Samaritan woman comes to the well, and she's shocked when Jesus begins talking to her because, first, the Jews and Samaritans bitterly hated each other and, secondly, she's a woman. In this culture, it would've been beneath a rabbi to speak to an unfamiliar woman in public. Not only that, but she's likely an outcast among her people because both the time and manner of her being at the well are culturally unusual. She comes to the well alone, without the company of several other women, and around noon ("about the sixth hour"[162]), a very hot part of the day when it's likely no one else would be there. We find out why she's a pariah not from her, but from Jesus.

First, let me point out that we see both Jesus' human and divine natures come into play here. We see Jesus' humanity in that he's tired and thirsty, it being the hot part of the day. But we see Jesus' divinity when Jesus tells her to go get her husband, and when she says she has no husband, Jesus – being the omnipresent, all-knowing God – tells her,

"You are right in saying, 'I have no husband'; for you have had five husbands, and the one you now have is not your husband. What you have said is true." (John 4:17-18)

We don't know the specifics of this woman's life, but it's clear she's an outsider among the Samaritans because of a spotty history and her current immoral life of living with a man she isn't married to. The woman replies,

"Sir, I perceive that you are a prophet. Our fathers worshiped on this mountain, but you say that in Jerusalem is the place where people ought to worship." (John 4:19-20)

---

[162] John 4:6.

What the woman is referring to here is a religious dispute between Jews and Samaritans, who were half-breed Jews. The Jews worshipped at the Temple in Jerusalem in Judea, but the Samaritans worshipped on Mount Gerizim in Samaria. Samaritans also considered only the first five books of the Old Testament scripture.

Jesus says several things to her in response, but for the moment, we only need to be concerned with one:

You worship what you do not know; we worship what we know, for salvation is from the Jews. (John 4:22)

Notice what Jesus did *not* say. He didn't say, "We worship in Jerusalem; you worship on Mount Garizim. No big deal! There are many paths to God!" Nor did Jesus say, "I follow the Jewish faith, and you follow the Samaritans faith, but your heart is in the right place, so I think you're saved from sin." No, Jesus didn't say any such sort of things. He said, "You worship what you do not know" and "salvation is from the Jews." The Jews worship "what we know," because God had revealed it to them. God had given to them the only true religion, which Jesus would fulfill[163] and perfect.[164]

Jesus didn't confirm her false faith or give approval of her following a corruption of Judaism; he – without any room for doubt – told her she was following a false religion. Of course doing this nowadays isn't considered polite or politically correct, but what is more loving – letting someone die in their sins or telling them about the one, true way to salvation?

Now, also notice what else Jesus does *not* do. He doesn't talk to the woman rudely. He doesn't talk to this outcast woman as if she is below

---

[163] Matthew 5:17.
[164] Hebrews 12:2.

him. He doesn't talk to this morally weak woman like she's dumb. Disagreement doesn't have to be degrading.

Before we move on, let's just look at what else Jesus said to her:

"Woman, believe me, the hour is coming when neither on this mountain [Mt. Gerizim] nor in Jerusalem will you worship the Father. You worship what you do not know; we worship what we know, for salvation is from the Jews. But the hour is coming, and is now here, when the true worshipers will worship the Father in spirit and truth, for the Father is seeking such people to worship him. God is spirit, and those who worship him must worship in spirit and truth."
(John 4:21-24)

Jesus is bringing a new era into God's salvation history, a new era of worship, where people will no longer worship at the Temple in Jerusalem, but they'll worship God wherever they are in "spirit and truth." Thousands of years ago, God chose the Jewish people to be his representative people on the earth, to introduce salvation to the world, and now Jesus, the Jewish Messiah, is ushering in the new age: *"the hour is coming, and is now here."* The Son of God has come to fulfill the Old Testament by dying on a cross for the sins of those who would believe, bringing in a new era where God's people will expand past the Jews, and they'll no longer need to give sacrifices for their sins at the Temple. Through Jesus' work, God will join his people ("true worshipers") with him in a new way through the Holy Spirit dwelling in them.

And Jesus invites this fallen woman – a Samaritan, an opponent to the Jews – to join in. And what does she do? She immediately leaves her water jar and goes into town, inviting others to come meet Jesus.

Those bumper stickers where the word "COEXIST" is spelled out with religious symbols of many different world religions are very popular where I live, and *tolerance* is a word a lot of people are concerned with these days. Jesus would agree that all religions should coexist *in peace*, but he wouldn't agree that they *should all exist*. He would disagree that they're all correct or true because he came to proclaim the one true religion and to snatch souls from Hell. All followers of Jesus should speak truth in love,[165] but speaking truth in love doesn't mean indiscriminately accepting everything another person chooses. Likewise, to withhold the truth because of "love" is not loving at all.

Let's put it another way: Does "I disagree with you" mean "I hate you"? Of course not. Disagreement does not equal hate. If it were the case that disagreement meant hatred, no marriage would have any hope of lasting past the first week. In fact, no relationship would lead to marriage nor would any friendship last! Despite what some want you to believe, disagreement can be because of love, and disagreement can be given in a loving way. "Tolerance" is respecting those you disagree with. That is the very definition of tolerance. Tolerance is not blindly affirming every opinion every person holds. Such mentality only leads to absurdity and chaos because differing opinions (and religions) contradict each other, and where there are contradictions, everyone can't be right.

Often when someone starts throwing around accusations of intolerance, what they're really saying is "I don't like your opinion," and instead of respectfully opening a dialogue with the other person, they simply label that person bigoted or stupid. Disagreement doesn't make one intolerant; dehumanizing someone through name-calling and refusing to respectfully consider their views is intolerant.

Jesus had all the ammunition he needed to tear this Samaritan woman down. But, instead, he lovingly corrected her, gave her the truth, and invited her to join him.

---

[165] Ephesians 4:15.

Only Jesus Could Win Us Salvation

Christians are often accused of being arrogant or pompous for claiming Jesus is the only way to salvation. Sadly, these accusations are sometimes justified. We all know of Christians who have - quite ironically - communicated their faith in the God of Peace in unloving ways. But simply communicating something you believe is truth (whether it's a popular truth or not) isn't arrogant within itself, and it doesn't have to be done in a haughty manner. In fact, it *should not* be done in such a manner because no Christian has ever earned his or her own salvation (as we discussed last chapter) and, thus, no one has reason to be proud, arrogant, or boastful.[166] Yet sometimes even Christians who express in a humble manner their belief that Jesus is the only way to salvation are accused of being arrogant or close-minded.

Despite the messiness that sometimes comes with expressing the belief that Jesus is the only way, answering the question *Why is following Jesus the only way to salvation?* is relatively simple: Because only Jesus could accomplish saving us from our sins. Why? Because only Jesus is fully human and fully God.[167] Unlike Jesus, no other person in history can say he's uniquely God and man. And Jesus being both human and God was absolutely necessary for winning salvation for fallen mankind.

FULLY HUMAN

First, let's look at why Jesus being human is important for our salvation. In his *Systematic Theology*,[168] Wayne Grudem explains that Jesus being *fully human* is absolutely necessary for the salvation of the world so Jesus could...

---

[166] Ephesians 2:8-9
[167] The hypostatic union!
[168] See Chapter 26:"The Person of Christ" in *Systematic Theology* by Wayne Grudem.

Who Jesus Ain't

(1) Represent humankind while living in complete obedience to God.

Sin and death entered the world through Adam, the first man, when he and Eve willfully disobeyed God:[169]

Therefore, just as sin came into the world through one man, and death through sin, and so death spread to all men because all sinned. (Romans 5:12)

But Jesus, as a human, is able to represent us and undo what Adam started:

For as by the one man's disobedience the many were made sinners, so by the one man's obedience the many will be made righteous. (Romans 5:19)

(2) Be a substitute sacrifice.

Hebrews 10 tells us that the Old Testament law, including the Jewish sacrificial system, is *"a shadow of the good things to come"*[170] because *"it is impossible for the blood of bulls and goats to take away sins."*[171] Jesus said he came not to do away with the Old Testament law, but to fulfill it,[172] and he fulfilled the Jewish sacrificial system by his death on the cross, so those who believe *"have been sanctified through the offering of the body of Jesus Christ once for all."*[173] Don't overlook that important phrase at the end of that last sentence: *"once for all."* Hebrews 10 goes on to tell us that the Jewish priests go on giving daily

---

[169] See Genesis 3.

[170] Hebrews 10:1.

[171] Hebrews 10:4.

[172] Matthew 5:17.

[173] Hebrews 10:10.

sacrifices *"which can never take away sins,"*[174] but Jesus *"offered for all time a single sacrifice for sins."*[175]

Grudem writes, "If Jesus had not been man, he could not have died in our place and paid the penalty that was due to us."

(3) Be the mediator between God and humans.

"We needed a mediator who could represent us to God and who could represent God to us," Grudem writes. Only the God-man Jesus could fulfill this role. Paul, the writer of 1 Timothy, would agree:

For there is one God, and there is one mediator between God and men, the man Christ Jesus, who gave himself as a ransom for all, which is the testimony given at the proper time. (1 Timothy 2:5-6)

(4) Fulfill God's original purpose for man to rule over creation in obedience to God.

We see this original purpose given by God after he created humankind:

And God blessed them. And God said to them, "Be fruitful and multiply and fill the earth and subdue it, and have dominion over the fish of the sea and over the birds of the heavens and over every living thing that moves on the earth." (Genesis 1:28)

Humans, made in God's image, are to be God's representatives on Earth and be caretakers and stewards of the earth in God's name. Sadly, this mandate given to humans by God has been frustrated and deferred by humanity's rebellion and fall into sin.

---

[174] Hebrews 10:11.
[175] Hebrews 10:12.

(5) & (6) Be our example and pattern in this life, and in our future redeemed bodies.

If Jesus were not truly human, he couldn't have served as an example for us to follow:

[Jesus said,] For I have given you an example, that you also should do just as I have done to you. (John 13:15)

For to this you have been called, because Christ also suffered for you, leaving you an example, so that you might follow in his steps. (1 Peter 2:21)

(7) And sympathize with us as our high priest.

If Jesus were not fully man, how could he truly relate to us? How could he go to God for us as our perfect priest?

For we do not have a high priest who is unable to sympathize with our weaknesses, but one who in every respect has been tempted as we are, yet without sin. Let us then with confidence draw near to the throne of grace, that we may receive mercy and find grace to help in time of need. (Hebrews 4:15-16)

Take note: Jesus is *still* a man, even after his resurrection and ascension into Heaven,[176] and he will remain a man forever. Grudem writes,

> "Jesus did not temporarily become man, but his
> divine nature was permanently united to his human
> nature, and he lives forever not just as the eternal Son
> of God, the second person of the Trinity, but also as
> Jesus, the man who was born of Mary, and as Christ,

---

[176] Acts 1:6-11.

171

Messiah and Savior of his people. Jesus will remain
fully God and fully man, yet one person, forever."

FULLY DIVINE

Before we move on, let's also quickly look at how Jesus being *fully
God* is absolutely necessary for our salvation. Grudem lays this out
in his *Systematic Theology* as well. It's essential for Jesus to be fully
God because...

**(1) Only someone who is infinite God could bear the full penalty for
all the sins of all those who would believe in him.**

No finite creature could ever take on the weight of all the sins of all
those saved by Jesus.

*He himself bore our sins in his body on the tree, that we might die to
sin and live to righteousness. By his wounds you have been healed.
(1 Peter 2:24)*

**(2) Scripture is undeniably clear that salvation only comes from God
himself.**

For example, Jonah declares, "*Salvation belongs to the LORD*,"[177] not
from any human being or creature.

**(3) And again, only a God-man can be mediator between God
and mankind.**

---

[177] Jonah 2:9.

Who Jesus Ain't

Only someone fully God and fully man can both bring us back to God, speak on our behalf to God, and also fully reveal God to us.[178]

Grudem writes, "Thus, if Jesus is not fully God, we have no salvation and ultimately no Christianity. It is no accident that throughout history those groups that have given up belief in the full deity of Christ have not remained long within the Christian faith..."

In Jesus' dual nature, we see the utter uniqueness of Jesus of Nazareth and, therefore, Christianity. Everything about Jesus is unique, from his conception and birth, to his sinless life, to his claims and his promises, to his resurrection and ascension, and to his fully human and fully divine natures.

Since Jesus is God, he could bear the full penalty of all the sins of the world. Since Jesus is human, he could represent us. Only the God-man could live a sinless life, and only by living a sinless life in perfect obedience to God the Father could someone be an adequate, perfect, and undeserving sacrificial substitution for the forgiveness of our sins.

So, now is a good time to read one of the most famous pieces about Jesus ever written:

For God so loved the world, that he gave his only Son, that whoever believes in him should not perish but have eternal life. For God did not send his Son into the world to condemn the world, but in order that the world might be saved through him. Whoever believes in him is not condemned, but whoever does not believe is condemned already, because he has not believed in the name of the only Son of God. (John 3:16-18)

---

[178] See Hebrews 4:15-16 again.

Who Jesus Ain't

Exclusive Claims of Jesus' First Followers

So, did Jesus' first followers think he was the only way to God and salvation? As we saw above in those quotes from the New Testament, the answer is "yes." As Peter, filled with the Holy Spirit, declares in Acts 4,

...let it be known to all of you and to all the people of Israel that by the name of Jesus Christ of Nazareth, whom you crucified, whom God raised from the dead – by him this [formally crippled] man is standing before you well. This Jesus is the stone that was rejected by you, the builders, which has become the cornerstone. And there is salvation in no one else, for there is no other name under heaven given among men by which we must be saved. (Acts 4:10-12)

Exclusive Claims of Jesus Himself

Did Jesus make exclusive claims about himself? Really, we only have to look at *one* statement by Jesus to answer this. However, I think at this point you understand that much of what Jesus did and said was exclusively unique.

But let's look quickly at what's often called the *Seven "I AM" Statements* of Jesus from the Gospel of John. We already looked at when Jesus claimed the divine name of God (Yahweh) by saying, "I AM" in **John 8:58**,[179] almost getting himself stoned for blasphemy. But let's look at seven more "I AM" statements of Jesus (in order of appearance, switching the last two so we can end with the most explicit):

---

[179] See Chapter 8 of this book.

Who Jesus Ain't

The 7 Exclusive "I AM" Statements of Jesus

#1 - John 6:35
Jesus said to them, "I am the bread of life; whoever comes to me shall not hunger, and whoever believes in me shall never thirst."

#2 - John 8:12
Again Jesus spoke to them, saying, "I am the light of the world. Whoever follows me will not walk in darkness, but will have the light of life."

#3 & 4 - John 10:9 & 11
*So Jesus again said to them, "Truly, truly, I say to you, I am the door of the sheep. All who came before me are thieves and robbers, but the sheep did not listen to them. **I am the door. If anyone enters by me, he will be saved and will go in and out and find pasture.** The thief comes only to steal and kill and destroy. I came that they may have life and have it abundantly. **I am the good shepherd. The good shepherd lays down his life for the sheep.** He who is a hired hand and not a shepherd, who does not own the sheep, sees the wolf coming and leaves the sheep and flees, and the wolf snatches them and scatters them. He flees because he is a hired hand and cares nothing for the sheep. I am the good shepherd. I know my own and my own know me, just as the Father knows me and I know the Father; and I lay down my life for the sheep. (10:9-15)*

#5 - John 11:25
*Jesus said to her, "I am the resurrection and the life. **Whoever believes in me, though he die, yet shall he live,** and everyone who lives and believes in me shall never die..." (11:25-26)*

#6 - John 15:1
I am the true vine, and my Father is the vinedresser. *Every branch in me that does not bear fruit he takes away, and every branch that does bear fruit he prunes, that it may bear more fruit. (15:1-2)*

#7- John 14:6
Jesus said to him, "I am the way, and the truth, and the life. No one comes to the Father except through me."

One More Thought

Jesus died a horribly brutal death on a Roman cross for the sake of all those who would believe in him to be saved from their sins. Jesus did this willingly, yet also prayed in the Garden of Gethsemane before his arrest and crucifixion, *"Abba, Father, all things are possible for you. Remove this cup from me. Yet not what I will, but what you will."*[180] God the Son went *willingly* to the cross, but he also was well aware of the high price he would pay to complete the task he became flesh to accomplish. In Gethsemane, he essentially asks God the Father, *If there's any other way to accomplish salvation, then please spare me from the horrible death of the cross.* But there is no other way, and he goes willingly.

Jesus of Nazareth was literally tortured. The flesh was ripped from his back by the metal pieces woven into a Roman whip. Then, with that same shredded body, already losing much blood, he carried his cross to the place of his death. Spikes were driven through his wrists and feet – spikes that literally held the weight of his body as the cross was set upright. Then, the slow death began. Hanging naked in the desert sun, the weight of his body made it hard to breathe. Hanging by his outstretched arms, shocks of pain shot through his shoulders as they possibly dislocated. Until finally – perhaps going into shock due to blood loss and his heart giving out – he breathed his last.

Here's the thing: If salvation could be won by any other way, then Jesus didn't have to die. If there were *any other way* – even *one* – for God to accomplish salvation from sin, Jesus died for nothing. In other words, if

---

[180] Mark 14:36.

there were a Plan B for saving the world from sin other than Jesus dying on the cross, Jesus wouldn't have died on the cross. He would've said, "See Plan B." And if Jesus' death on the cross were Plan B, he would've said, "Plan A works just fine."

We also have this issue: if there were any other way for God the Father to reconnect with his created people and overlook their sins, and God the Father *still* put Jesus to death on the cross, then Jesus' death was needless brutality. In other words, if God the Father knew forgiveness of sins could be achieved through humans simply following some rules or completing some rituals or being "nice" or doing X, Y, and Z, why would God the Son need to become a man and die? If pluralism and universalism are true, then God the Father and God the Son both made extremely illogical decisions to allow an act of absolute brutality for absolutely no reason whatsoever.

Is Jesus a Universalist or a pluralist? No, or else he wouldn't have given his life. But he knew it was the only way.

CHAPTER 13: JESUS AIN'T A HIPPY OR YOUR HOMEBOY (OR A WIMP)

It's easy to see why some people think of Jesus of Nazareth as some harmless hippy. Usually he's portrayed in paintings with long, flowing hair and sandals. We know Jesus taught a message of peace and love. He even loves children,[181] and he admits he's "gentle and lowly in heart."[182]

Because of this, it's also easy to see Jesus as a wimp. I mean – come on – how tough can that bathrobe-wearing guy cuddling a lamb in the painting be? How many tough hippies do you know? In fact, how tough can someone look while his emaciated body hangs on a crucifix? For

---

[181] Matthew 19:14.
[182] Matthew 11:29.

Who Jesus Ain't

God-in-the-flesh, Jesus doesn't come across all that powerful; he couldn't even stop his own beating and crucifixion, and he had no answer to this challenge as he hung dying on the cross:

And the people stood by, watching, but the rulers scoffed at him, saying, "He saved others; let him save himself, if he is the Christ of God, his Chosen One!" The soldiers also mocked him, coming up and offering him sour wine and saying, "If you are the King of the Jews, save yourself!" (Luke 23: 35-37)

Jesus may not have been a tough or powerful guy, but he was certainly a nice guy. The sort of guy you'd like to hang out with. Even though I was never a hippy myself, all hippy-types I've known have always been pleasant, easy-going, and accepting to all. Jesus seems like he would make a good drinking buddy or roommate. We even see in the Gospels that he befriended the outcasts of society, like prostitutes and tax collectors. A popular T-shirt with high school and college students even proclaims, "Jesus is my homeboy."

Is this understanding of Jesus accurate?

The problem is, we often try to make Jesus into a one-dimensional person. No human – including anyone reading this book – is a one-dimensional person. So, why do we try to make the eternal Son of God one-dimensional? Trust me, he's infinitely more complex than any human being!

Jesus certainly taught love and compassion. In the Sermon on the Mount,[183] he even teaches against insulting others.[184] In this passage, the Greek word often translated "insults" is "raca," which is specifically a term of abuse, a term that degrades people. "Raca" suggests that the person insulted has no value. Jesus teaches against dehumanizing

---

[183] Matthew 5-7.
[184] Matthew 5:21-26.

others. To dehumanize someone is to not recognize that person as an image-bearer of God.[185]

In fact, Jesus equates this sort of anger and hatred of others to murder. Before murder becomes a physical act, people often "murder" others in their mind (and with their mouths) by dehumanizing them:

You have heard that it was said to those of old, 'You shall not murder; and whoever murders will be liable to judgment.' But I say to you that everyone who is angry with his brother will be liable to judgment; whoever insults his brother will be liable to the council; and whoever says, 'You fool!' will be liable to the hell of fire. (Matthew 5:21-22)

Along with the above teachings, we also have Jesus' commands to love your neighbor as yourself,[186] to love your enemies and pray for those who persecute you,[187] and to even do good for those who hate you,[188] all commands Jesus highlights in the famous Parable of the Good Samaritan.[189]

But Jesus is not your beatnik cousin or your hipster roommate. He's one of the persons of the Triune God of Scripture, which means Jesus is God. We already looked at how Jesus is God in an earlier chapter, but let's look at two other verses:

For by him all things were created, in heaven and on earth, visible and invisible, whether thrones or dominions or rulers or authorities – all things were created through him and for him. And he is before all things, and in him all things hold together. (Colossians 1:16-17)

---

[185] Genesis 1:27.
[186] Mark 12:31 (Also see Leviticus 19:18).
[187] Matthew 5:44.
[188] Luke 6:27.
[189] Luke 10:25-37.

Who Jesus Ain't

He is the radiance of the glory of God and the exact imprint of his
nature, and he upholds the universe by the word of his power.
(Hebrews 1:3)

In these two verses we read about what Grudem calls Jesus'
preservation, which is part of God's providence over his creation. He
explains it as "God keeps all created things existing and maintaining
the properties with which he created them" with "active, purposeful
control." He writes, "God, in preserving all things he had made, also
causes them to maintain the properties with which he created them,"
and if God didn't do this, then "all except the triune God would
instantly cease to exist."[190]

So, not only did Jesus, God the Son, create all things, but he holds all
things together. He keeps the solar system spinning; he keeps gravity
working; he keeps your heart beating. This doesn't sound like
powerlessness to me.

Moreover, as we discussed earlier in this book, the Bible confirms that
God is a Trinity – God the Father, God the Son, and God the Holy
Spirit. This means Jesus is the same God who in the Old Testament
flooded the earth with water to wipe out much of sinful humanity,
destroyed the abominable Sodom and Gomorrah, commanded the
ancient Israelites to wipe out the evil Canaanites, and took the lives of
every firstborn of Egypt because of the Pharaoh's stubborn refusal to set
Israel free from slavery.

At the same time, Jesus is the same God who in the Old Testament
showed grace and mercy by sending Jonah to pagan Nineveh to warn
them to repent (which they did) or be destroyed,[191] who vowed to
Abraham not to destroy Sodom if only ten righteous men lived

---

[190] Chapter 16: "God's Providence" in *Systematic Theology* by Wayne Grudem.
[191] See the Book of Jonah.

within it,[192] who sent two angels to rescue Lot and his family from Sodom before its imminent destruction, whose fatherly love clothed Adam and Eve even as he evicted them from Eden due to their sin,[193] and who even protected Cain from attack after he became the world's first murderer.[194]

Personally, my favorite example of God's power (and righteous wrath) is in Exodus at the Red Sea. After begrudgingly releasing Israel from slavery, Pharaoh changes his mind and sends his army to slaughter them. Israel finds itself trapped between Pharaoh's army and the Red Sea with nowhere to escape. When the people of Israel began whining, asking why Moses had led them out into the wilderness only to die and saying that they were better off staying as slaves in Egypt, Moses says,

"Fear not, stand firm, and see the salvation of the Lord, which he will work for you today. For the Egyptians whom you see today, you shall never see again. The Lord will fight for you, and you have only to be silent." (Exodus 14:13)

Thus, God parts the Red Sea and Israel flees through it on dry ground. Then, safely on the opposite shore, Israel watches as Pharaoh's army, still within the sea, pursues them, and God brings the sea back together, utterly destroying Pharaoh's army.

While celebrating what God has done for them, Moses and the people of Israel compose a song praising God, which is recorded in the Bible. Here are the opening lines:

"I will sing to the LORD, for he has triumphed gloriously;
*   the horse and his rider he has thrown into the sea.*
The LORD is my strength and my song,

---

[192] Genesis 18.
[193] Genesis 3:21.
[194] Genesis 4:14-15.

and he has become my salvation;
this is my God, and I will praise him,
*   my father's God, and I will exalt him.*
The LORD is a man of war;
*   the LORD is his name. (Exodus 15:1-3)*

God, and thus Jesus, is not your homeboy. Jesus is to be honored, respected, praised, worshiped, and even feared. Notice the second to the last line in the quote from the song above: "The LORD is a man of war." Now, the Bible translation I use regularly – for teaching, personal reading, and even seminary studying – is the ESV translation of the Bible, but for this line I prefer how the NIV and NASB translate it:

"The LORD is a warrior."

What an awesome statement! The LORD is a warrior! Here are five more reasons why Jesus is a warrior:

1. JESUS AIN'T AFRAID OF CONFRONTATION

A lot of people hate confrontations and do everything they can to avoid them, but Jesus confronted his hostile adversaries not by passive-aggressively talking about them to others or by writing scathing things about them or even by cyber-bullying them over social media, but he confronted them face-to-face. Not only that, he silenced them. These are not the actions of a coward or weakling.

The chief priests, scribes, Pharisees, and Sadducee were out to get Jesus, but Jesus never avoided a debate with them. As we saw earlier in this book in Chapter 11, Jesus never shied away from speaking the hard truth to them about their hypocrisy and empty religion.

In **Matthew 10:16**, Jesus warns his disciples,

"Behold, I am sending you out as sheep in the midst of wolves, so be wise as serpents and innocent as doves."

In Jesus' debates with the religious leaders of his day, we see Jesus model this teaching again and again. For instance, in **Luke 20**, Luke records three attempts by the religious leaders to outsmart, trap, and repudiate Jesus. After three failed attempts – after the religious leaders are left speechless by Jesus' rebuttals three times – Luke tells us,

For they no longer dared to ask him any question. (Luke 20:40)

2. JESUS AIN'T AFRAID OF DEMONS

Not only is Jesus not afraid of demons, but the demons tremble at the sound of his name! **James 2:19** tells us:

You believe that God is one; you do well. Even the demons believe – and shudder!

It's convicting to us today to think demons actually understand God with a better sense of fear and reverence than we do! They have good reason. Scripture shows us that casting out demons was a regular part of Jesus' ministry:

Whenever the unclean spirits saw Him, they would fall down before Him and shout, "You are the Son of God!" (Mark 3:11)

While the sun was setting, all those who had any who were sick with various diseases brought them to Him; and laying His hands on each one of them, He was healing them. Demons also were coming out of many, shouting, "You are the Son of God!" But rebuking them, He would not allow them to speak, because they knew Him to be the Christ. (Luke 4:40-41)

Who Jesus Ain't

Just then there was a man in their synagogue with an unclean spirit; and he cried out, saying, "What business do we have with each other, Jesus of Nazareth? Have You come to destroy us? I know who You are – the Holy One of God!" And Jesus rebuked him, saying, "Be quiet, and come out of him!" Throwing him into convulsions, the unclean spirit cried out with a loud voice and came out of him. They were all amazed, so that they debated among themselves, saying, "What is this? A new teaching with authority! He commands even the unclean spirits, and they obey Him." (Mark 1:23-27)

Notice how Jesus isn't even seeking out the demons. His presence is enough to throw them into a fit of panic and terror, and Jesus has absolute control over them. Likely the most famous case of demon-possession within Scripture is probably so because it's the worst case of demon-possession recorded in the Gospels:

They came to the other side of the sea, to the country of the Gerasenes. And when Jesus had stepped out of the boat, immediately there met him out of the tombs a man with an unclean spirit. He lived among the tombs. And no one could bind him anymore, not even with a chain, for he had often been bound with shackles and chains, but he wrenched the chains apart, and he broke the shackles in pieces. No one had the strength to subdue him. Night and day among the tombs and on the mountains he was always crying out and cutting himself with stones. And when he saw Jesus from afar, he ran and fell down before him. And crying out with a loud voice, he said, "What have you to do with me, Jesus, Son of the Most High God? I adjure you by God, do not torment me." (Mark 5:1-7)

The demon-possessed man tells Jesus his name is *"Legion, for we are many,"*[195] presumably because a whole legion of demons are within him. Yet even they fear Jesus, and even this poor, tormented man is freed at Jesus' command.

---

[195] Mark 5:9.

Jesus' disciples were also able to cast out demons in his name (by his authority).[196] In one of the more entertaining incidences in the New Testament, **Acts 19** tells of some Jewish exorcists attempting to use Jesus' name to repel evil spirits, but not doing so successfully:

And the evil spirit answered and said to them, "I recognize Jesus, and I know about Paul, but who are you?" And the man, in whom was the evil spirit, leaped on them and subdued all of them and overpowered them, so that they fled out of that house naked and wounded. (Acts 19:15-16)

In fact, Jesus just isn't intimidated by demons, he's not scared of Satan either. In **John 14:30**, Jesus says Satan (*"the ruler of this world"*) has *"no claim on me."* When Satan tries to tempt Jesus away from his ministry, Jesus easily rebukes him by quoting Scripture.[197] When Jesus hears of the good work his disciples are doing, he states that he has seen Satan fall.[198] When the Pharisees claim Jesus is casting out demons by the name of Beelzebul, the supposed ruler of the demons, Jesus logically points out the absurdity of using Satan's forces against Satan's forces, and states,

But if I cast out demons by the Spirit of God, then the kingdom of God has come upon you. Or how can anyone enter the strong man's house and carry off his property, unless he first binds the strong man? And then he will plunder his house. (Matthew 12:28-29)

Biblical scholars agree that "the strong man" here in Jesus' metaphor is Satan. Jesus has bound Satan, and Jesus is robbing his "house." He is snatching the souls of sinners from Satan's hands! Jesus delivered Satan's deathblow on the cross, where sin and death received mortal wounds. Now, Satan, sin, and death are in their death throes, reeling

---

[196] See Luke 10:17, for example.
[197] Matthew 4:1-11.
[198] Luke 10:18.

from that blow, and they will finally be done away with completely at Jesus' Second Coming.[199] As Paul writes to Jesus' followers in **Romans 16:20,**

The God of peace will soon crush Satan under your feet.

3. JESUS AIN'T SOFT ON SIN

Often people critical of Christians' outspokenness about certain moral issues point to Jesus spending time with prostitutes, corrupt tax collectors, and other obvious sinners as a reason for Christians to not be "judgmental." The same people love to quote the words of Jesus himself from **Matthew 7:1**:

Judge not, that you be not judged.

These critics of Christianity are partially right. Jesus did spend a lot of time with sinners (which we all are), but their mistake is in thinking Jesus was all right with their sins. Jesus spent time with sinners to share with them his message of salvation. Do these critics of Christians really think Jesus just hung out with, say, prostitutes and didn't hope to lead them away from a life of sin? Do they really think that God the Son grabbed lunch with swindling tax collectors and then said, "Go on exploiting your position and stealing money from people. Who am I to judge?" Instead, Jesus says to one man,

Sin no more, that nothing worse may happen to you. (John 5:14)

Likewise, upon hearing about some Galileans who had been killed by Pontius Pilate, Jesus has an unexpected response. He says,

---

[199] See Revelation 20.

Who Jesus Ain't

"Do you think that these Galileans were worse sinners than all the other Galileans, because they suffered in this way? No, I tell you; but unless you repent, you will all likewise perish. Or those eighteen on whom the tower in Siloam fell and killed them: do you think that they were worse offenders than all the others who lived in Jerusalem? No, I tell you; but unless you repent, you will all likewise perish." (Luke 13:1-5)

Those who told him about the killings probably were surprised by this response; they probably told Jesus this because they thought he might be the Messiah and expected him to lead the Jews in revolt against the Romans. They probably were waiting for him to start bad-mouthing the Romans. Instead, Jesus takes the opportunity to talk about sin.

Or maybe they told Jesus about the Galileans being killed because they thought the Galileans were punished in this way due to them being sinners. Perhaps some Jews thought that when the tower of Siloam (likely a tower along the walls of Jerusalem) collapsed and killed eighteen people, that this was God punishing them for their sins. Either way, Jesus' response is not ambiguous, and it isn't to confirm that these dead people must have been worse sinners than others, but to point out that they were no worse sinners than the rest of us, and if we all don't repent of our sins – if we don't turn from our sins and ask for God's forgiveness – we're all going to be judged and perish. That doesn't sound like something a hippy would say.

Jesus also said,

"I tell you, my friends, do not fear those who kill the body, and after that have nothing more that they can do. But I will warn you whom to fear: fear him who, after he has killed, has authority to cast into hell. Yes, I tell you, fear him! (Luke 12:4-5)

Who has authority to cast into hell? God alone. Who will judge all sinners, alive and dead, at his Second Coming? Jesus, God the Son.

Who Jesus Ain't

No, Jesus didn't easily dismiss sin.

Furthermore, let's look at *all* of Jesus' words in Matthew 7:

Judge not, that you be not judged. For with the judgment you pronounce you will be judged, and with the measure you use it will be measured to you. Why do you see the speck that is in your brother's eye, but do not notice the log that is in your own eye? Or how can you say to your brother, 'Let me take the speck out of your eye,' when there is the log in your own eye? You hypocrite, first take the log out of your own eye, and then you will see clearly to take the speck out of your brother's eye. (Matthew 7:1-5)

And *immediately* after, in the very next verse, Jesus says this shockingly judgmental statement as well:

Do not give dogs what is holy, and do not throw your pearls before pigs, lest they trample them underfoot and turn to attack you. (Matthew 7:6)

R. T. France in his commentary on Matthew explains that in 7:6 Jesus is telling the disciples to "be discriminating" in what they share with certain people so "as not to lay them open to abuse."[200] In other words, Jesus is telling them to use their judgment and, essentially, don't waste their time with certain people. I often keep this verse in mind when a skeptic engages me online; if it becomes clear that the skeptic is not interested in a respectful and honest dialogue, I move on. So, yes, the same Jesus who tells you to love your enemies and to pray for those who persecute you,[201] and the same Jesus who tells you you're liable for

---

[200] *The Gospel of Matthew* (The New International Commentary on the New Testament) by R. T. France (William B. Eerdmans Publishing Company, 2007).

[201] Matthew 5:48.

judgment and hell for insulting your brothers,[202] also tells you not to "throw your pearls to pigs."

So, in this famously often-misquoted "judge not" verse of Matthew 7, Jesus isn't speaking against all judgment. He's speaking against harsh and hypocritical judgment. (Let's be logical: it's utterly impossible to not use judgment. Even those saying Christians are judgmental are judging Christians!) Jesus says to first take the log out of your own eye, before you do what? Before you take the speck out of your brother's eye!

Jesus is saying to take care of your own garbage before you go speaking to others about their garbage. Jesus is not condemning all judgment, but he's telling us to do it in the right way. We're to speak truth in love, not harshly or hypocritically, and the only way to do that correctly is to make sure you're in a good place yourself, which to Christians mean living as closely to God as possible. All Christians are sinners saved by God's grace;[203] this is something we must never forget when interacting with unbelievers. Even when correcting the sin of others, whether the sins of unbelievers or fellow Christians, we must always remain humble because we're all sinners.

This is important to note: Jesus had no log to remove from his eye. Jesus is the sinless Son of God. If anyone were in the position to judge others, it's him – and he does. Jesus speaks about Hell more than anyone else in the entire Bible. More importantly, he was willingly tortured and experienced slow death on a Roman cross because of sin. If there's anyone who understands the seriousness of sin, it's Jesus of Nazareth.

---

[202] Matthew 5:22.
[203] Romans 3:23; Ephesians 2:8-9.

Jesus said, *"the truth will set you free."*[204] He spoke the truth in love even when people didn't want to hear it, because love without truth is useless sentimentality. Untruth does no one any good.

Furthermore, whoever thinks Jesus was always gentle and passive is forgetting the tense exchanges with the hypocritical religious leaders of his day we looked at earlier, where Jesus essentially gave them a verbal beat-down. If there's still any doubt about it, one incident tells us otherwise: How Jesus dealt with sinners who desecrated God's honor with greed in God's own Temple:

In the temple he found those who were selling oxen and sheep and pigeons, and the money-changers sitting there. And making a whip of cords, he drove them all out of the temple, with the sheep and oxen. And he poured out the coins of the money-changers and overturned their tables. And he told those who sold the pigeons, "Take these things away; do not make my Father's house a house of trade." His disciples remembered that it was written, "Zeal for your house will consume me."[205] *(John 2:14-17)*

This Jesus doesn't sound like the one-dimensional, passive wimp so many people want us to believe.

4. JESUS AIN'T GOING TO FORGIVE FOREVER

The person who told his followers to turn the other cheek won't be turning his cheek forever.

---

[204] John 8:32.
[205] Written in Psalm 69:9.

Who Jesus Ain't

What many don't realize about one of the most quoted passages of Scripture, *"For God so loved the world, that he gave his only Son, that whoever believes in him should not perish but have eternal life,"*[206] is that this open invitation for salvation will not be available forever. **John 3** goes on to tell us,

For God did not send his Son into the world to condemn the world, but in order that the world might be saved through him. Whoever believes in him is not condemned, but whoever does not believe is condemned already, because he has not believed in the name of the only Son of God. (John 3:17-18)

Notice the words "condemned already." In other words, Jesus isn't the reason people go to Hell to eternal separation from God; he's the reason people stay out of Hell. Many people get this backwards when they hear Christians say that Jesus is the only way to salvation. They think what's being said is, *Since you're not Christian, Jesus is condemning you to Hell.* Yet what Scripture teaches is, *You're already going to Hell, but Jesus is the solution.* We all have sin and are separated from God by it. God the Son could have chosen to (A) leave it this way or (B) become a man, absorb the punishment we deserve, and snatch us from Hell's grip by the free gift of salvation. Like all gifts, a person can only benefit from it if he receives the gift. Jesus isn't the cause but the cure.

But something else many don't understand about John 3 is that this gift of salvation is not an open offer forever. During Jesus' First Coming, he didn't come to condemn but to bring the free gift of salvation. In Jesus' Second Coming, he'll come as judge of the living and the dead,[207] bringing condemnation to all those who haven't repented and believed in what he accomplished on the cross.

---

[206] John 3:16.
[207] 1 Peter 4:5; 2 Timothy 4:1.

The apostle Paul speaks of Jesus judging the secrets of our hearts,[208] and he writes,

It is the Lord who judges me. Therefore do not pronounce judgment before the time, before the Lord comes, who will bring to light the things now hidden in darkness and will disclose the purposes of the heart. Then each one will receive his commendation from God. (1 Corinthians 4:4-5)

For we must all appear before the judgment seat of Christ, so that each one may receive what is due for what he has done in the body, whether good or evil. (2 Corinthians 5:10)

The Book of Revelation gives us both a glorious and horrifying vision of Jesus' return. For those who are of Jesus' flock, they don't have to fear condemnation because Jesus has stood in their place and taken their punishment, but those who aren't of Jesus' flock will be judged fairly, justly, and perfectly by the perfect, all-knowing Son of God, and apart from the saving power of Jesus' sacrifice, they'll all fall short.

5. JESUS AIN'T GOING EASY ON HIS ENEMIES

As we speak about Jesus not being a wimp, there's no better place to end than in the Book of Revelation, the last book of the Bible. During Jesus' Second Coming, he will declare war on all evil and destroy all his enemies, including Satan and death.[209] Those who rise up against him, in one last futile attempt at autonomy and rebellion, will meet a grisly defeat. The Book of Revelation is highly symbolic, so it's often difficult to know what to understand literally or symbolically. But whether it's to be understood literally or figuratively, the image painted in **Revelation 19** of the warrior Jesus returned to reclaim his creation is not for the

---

[208] Romans 2:16.
[209] Revelation 20.

faint of heart. As popular Christian rapper Shai Linne says in a song referring to this event: "Yeah, it's morbid, but it's fair."[210] Otherwise, I'll allow arguably the most graphic passage in the New Testament to speak for itself:

Then I saw heaven opened, and behold, a white horse! The one sitting on it is called Faithful and True, and in righteousness he judges and makes war. His eyes are like a flame of fire, and on his head are many diadems, and he has a name written that no one knows but himself. He is clothed in a robe dipped in blood, and the name by which he is called is The Word of God. And the armies of heaven, arrayed in fine linen, white and pure, were following him on white horses. From his mouth comes a sharp sword with which to strike down the nations, and he will rule them with a rod of iron. He will tread the winepress of the fury of the wrath of God the Almighty. On his robe and on his thigh he has a name written, King of kings and Lord of lords.

Then I saw an angel standing in the sun, and with a loud voice he called to all the birds that fly directly overhead, "Come, gather for the great supper of God, to eat the flesh of kings, the flesh of captains, the flesh of mighty men, the flesh of horses and their riders, and the flesh of all men, both free and slave, both small and great." And I saw the beast and the kings of the earth with their armies gathered to make war against him who was sitting on the horse and against his army. And the beast was captured, and with it the false prophet who in its presence had done the signs by which he deceived those who had received the mark of the beast and those who worshiped its image. These two were thrown alive into the lake of fire that burns with sulfur. And the rest were slain by the sword that came from the mouth of him who was sitting on the horse, and all the birds were gorged with their flesh. (Revelation 19:11-21)

---

[210] "Exalted (Psalm 110)" from the album *Lyrical Theology, Pt. 1: Theology* by Shai Linne (Lamp Mode Recordings, 2013).

Who Jesus Ain't

And So...

Jesus is not your hippy roommate or your homie or that pencil-necked nerd everyone used to push around. But Jesus also told his disciples this:

"This is my commandment, that you love one another as I have loved you. Greater love has no one than this, that someone lay down his life for his friends. You are my friends if you do what I command you. No longer do I call you servants, for the servant does not know what his master is doing; but I have called you friends, for all that I have heard from my Father I have made known to you. (John 15:12-15)

What a beautiful sentiment by the creator of the universe! And it's one that should deeply humble us – always remembering that God also said, *"my glory I give to no other."*[211]

---

[211] Isaiah 42:8.

CHAPTER 14: JESUS AIN'T A VICTIM

When we see a portrayal of Jesus hanging on the cross, punctured by metal spikes, whether in a famous painting, a movie, or in an ancient cathedral, it's easy to feel pity for him. Blood drips down his forehead from the crown of thorns. Often he looks frail and emaciated, his ribs showing through his skin. Some artists masterfully depict the sheer exhaustion from suffering on his face. We should feel pity for him because he truly suffered. But our pity must not bring us to think of Jesus as a victim.

Jesus ain't a hippy, your homeboy, a wimp, or a weakling, and he ain't a victim either.

Who Jesus Ain't

Jesus was *willingly* tortured and killed for the good of others – so you and I could be free from sin, no longer separated from God, and spend forever with him. He knew full well what he was getting into. He knew his mission and walked unwavering towards death. Have no doubt about it: Jesus was no passive victim. Jesus understood quite clearly for what purpose he became flesh, declaring,

For even the Son of Man came not to be served but to serve, and to give his life as a ransom for many. (Mark 10:45)

Throughout the Gospels, Jesus prophesies about his coming death. When some Pharisees and scribes ask Jesus for a sign from God, Jesus answers,

An evil and adulterous generation seeks for a sign, but no sign will be given to it except the sign of the prophet Jonah. For just as Jonah was three days and three nights in the belly of the great fish, so will the Son of Man be three days and three nights in the heart of the earth. (Matthew 12:39-40)

Here, Jesus is speaking of his death and burial in a tomb, and how three days later he will emerge from the tomb alive. Jesus made this even clearer to his own disciples:

And taking the twelve, he said to them, "See, we are going up to Jerusalem, and everything that is written about the Son of Man by the prophets will be accomplished. For he will be delivered over to the Gentiles and will be mocked and shamefully treated and spit upon. And after flogging him, they will kill him, and on the third day he will rise." But they understood none of these things. This saying was hidden from them, and they did not grasp what was said. (Luke 18:31-34)

Other than Jesus' actual accurate prediction of his mocking, flogging, death, and resurrection, we see two other interesting details here. First,

Who Jesus Ain't

Jesus speaks of his death also being written about by the Old Testament prophets. Secondly, we see Jesus' disciples utterly confused.

We're not going to explore the messianic prophecies of the Old Testament in this chapter since we touched on them in Chapter 6, but let's look again at parts of **Isaiah 52:13-53:12**, the famous prophecy about "The Suffering Servant," one more time to refresh our memories:

He was despised and rejected by men;
  a man of sorrows, and acquainted with grief;
and as one from whom men hide their faces
  he was despised, and we esteemed him not.
Surely he has borne our griefs
  and carried our sorrows;
yet we esteemed him stricken,
  smitten by God, and afflicted.
But he was pierced for our transgressions;
  he was crushed for our iniquities;
upon him was the chastisement that brought us peace,
  and with his wounds we are healed. (Isaiah 53:3-5)

Therefore I will divide him a portion with the many,
  and he shall divide the spoil with the strong,
because he poured out his soul to death
  and was numbered with the transgressors;
yet he bore the sin of many,
  and makes intercession for the transgressors. (Isaiah 53:12)

Keep in mind, Isaiah wrote this about 700 years before Jesus died on the cross for the sins of the world!

As we touched upon before quickly in Chapter 9, Jesus' disciples didn't understand completely who he was or what his mission was.[212] There

---

[212] For example, see Luke 18:31-34; John 14:1-9; Matthew 8:23-27.

was no expectation of a dying and rising Messiah, let alone one that was God in the flesh. Most of these Old Testament prophecies were a mystery or misunderstood until Jesus made them clear.

So, this is why we often find Jesus' disciples confused, even sometimes unintentionally getting in the way of Jesus' mission. After one of Jesus' pronouncements of his coming death, Peter, always the impulsive one, scolds Jesus for saying such things. In return, Jesus rebukes him right back, calling him "a hindrance" and even "Satan" for attempting to turn him away from his path to the cross![213] Ouch! (Again, where do we get this idea that Jesus was always sweet-tempered?)

Throughout the Gospels, we even see Jesus trying to keep his identity hidden.[214] Yes, he performs miracles as signs of who he is, but he also understands that he has to keep a lid on it to an extent until it's the right time for his death. The primary mission of Jesus of Nazareth was to die as a perfect sacrifice for the sin of humanity, but he had to first live a perfect life in obedience to God the Father and spread his good news. So, there's this tension in Jesus' ministry to proclaim that God's Kingdom has come, but at the same time not to proclaim it too loudly until the right time!

This is one of the main reasons Jesus primarily refers to himself as the Son of Man, the mysterious figure in **Daniel 7:13-14**.[215] If he came out calling himself the Messiah – who was understood to be a political figure and even a general, someone the Jews would expect to rid them of the Romans – the Roman Empire would've executed Jesus much sooner (as they did with other self-proclaimed "messiahs"). Likewise, if Jesus would've come out overtly declaring himself as God in the flesh, the Jewish religious leadership could've acted much faster with much more ammunition to condemn him. As it were, Jesus' ministry lasted

---

[213] Matthew 16:21-23.

[214] For example, see Mark 7:36 & 8:30 and Luke 4:41.

[215] See Chapter 9 of this book for more about Daniel 7 and the Son of Man.

only three years. Jesus walked a fine line of declaring that the Kingdom of God had come, and keeping it quiet until the right time.

John tells us in his gospel that it was when some Gentiles had come seeking Jesus that Jesus decided his ministry goals were met. Why? We can only speculate, but it seems likely that since Gentiles were seeking him out, his message had spread successfully throughout the Jewish people and further on to the non-Jews. Here, Jesus declares,

The hour has come for the Son of Man to be glorified. Truly, truly, I say to you, unless a grain of wheat falls into the earth and dies, it remains alone; but if it dies, it bears much fruit. (John 12:23-24)

Notice that Jesus' darkest hour is also where he'll be most glorified. The other Gospels tell us of Jesus' agony in the Garden of Gethsemane before his arrest, praying to God the Father, asking if there were another way and to spare him the cross. Yet, even in this very human moment, Jesus shows his willingness to die, saying three times,

My Father, if this cannot pass unless I drink it, your will be done. (Matthew 26:42)

Shortly after, Judas, the betrayer, arrives with others to arrest Jesus. Again, impulsive Peter gets in the way of Jesus completing his mission by drawing a sword and cutting off the ear of a servant of the high priest. Again, Jesus rebukes him:

"Put your sword back into its place. For all who take the sword will perish by the sword. Do you think that I cannot appeal to my Father, and he will at once send me more than twelve legions of angels? But how then should the Scriptures be fulfilled, that it must be so?" (Matthew 26:52-54)

Note again Jesus' reference to fulfilling Scripture, but most importantly for our purpose here, notice "twelve legions of angels" are at Jesus' disposal! The only reason he can be arrested and brought to the cross is because he has allowed it. Jesus is in total control the whole time. I once came across this quote attributed to an unknown samurai:

"Only a warrior chooses pacifism; others are condemned to it."

The idea here is that pacifism can only be truly practiced by someone with power to harm others. For example, if an 80-pound, 99-year-old woman is slapped and turns the other cheek, it's not as impressive as if a 220-pound, 22-year-old professional mixed martial arts fighter is slapped and turns the other cheek. The fighter was truly practicing pacifism because he has the power to harm. How much more is this true for the God who created the universe from nothing and destroyed the Egyptian army in the Red Sea?

It takes a certain kind of warrior to willingly go into battle knowing he will surely die. This is the type of warrior Jesus is. Yes, Jesus came humbly and lowly in spirit, but have no doubt that he still came as a warrior. These aren't the actions of a weakling, nor are the following words the words of a victim, but of one with authority over life and death:

I lay down my life that I may take it up again. No one takes it from me, but I lay it down of my own accord. (John 10:17)

CHAPTER 15: JESUS AIN'T AFRAID TO CRY

In this book, we've been exploring both Jesus of Nazareth's humanness and divineness. So, it'll be fitting to close this book by looking at an episode from Jesus' life recorded in **John 11** that beautifully displays both his human and divine natures: It's the popular story of Jesus raising Lazarus from the dead. Just knowing the basic events of the story alone make it a remarkable one. Lazarus dies, and Jesus comes and raises him from the grave before the eyes of his grieving family and friends. But by looking closer at some of the details, we'll get more insight into Jesus of Nazareth.

When word is sent to Jesus that Lazarus, a friend of Jesus' and the brother of Mary and Martha, is very sick, Jesus says,

Who Jesus Ain't

This illness does not lead to death. It is for the glory of God, so that the Son of God may be glorified through it. (John 11:4)

And then he waits *two whole days* longer before starting for Bethany, where Lazarus lives. Jesus' disciples don't think this is a good idea. After all, Bethany is close to Jerusalem, where Jesus had just escaped being stoned to death. Yet, Jesus won't be deterred, saying,

Lazarus has died, and for your sake I am glad that I was not there, so that you may believe. But let us go to him. (John 11:14)

So, here we see the purpose for Jesus going to raise Lazarus – and the reason for all of his miracles. Not only to glorify God, to bring God praise, but as signs that witness to who Jesus is so others may believe. Jesus' miracles aren't pointless works of wonder. They reveal God; they're God's self-disclosure, self-declaration. They're God's announcement that he is living and active.

When Jesus arrives, Lazarus has already been in a tomb for four days. This is significant because some rabbis taught that after death the soul would hover near the dead body trying to reenter it for three days, but after seeing the body's deterioration, the soul would finally depart. Thus, after three days, the Jews considered a person truly dead and beyond hope of return. After some interactions with Martha and Mary, Jesus goes to Lazarus' tomb:

Jesus said, "Take away the stone." Martha, the sister of the dead man, said to him, "Lord, by this time there will be an odor, for he has been dead four days." Jesus said to her, "Did I not tell you that if you believed you would see the glory of God?" So they took away the stone. And Jesus lifted up his eyes and said, "Father, I thank you that you have heard me. I knew that you always hear me, but I said this on account of the people standing around, that they may believe that you sent me." When he had said these things, he cried out with a loud voice, "Lazarus, come out." The man who had died came out,

his hands and feet bound with linen strips, and his face wrapped
with a cloth. Jesus said to them, "Unbind him, and let him go."
(John 11:39-44)

Ordering Lazarus alive after four days of being bound by death is just as
easy for Jesus as ordering Lazarus to be released from his grave-clothes,
the linens Jews wrapped their dead in. Undoubtedly, we see Jesus'
divinity in this event. As the omnipresent God, Jesus being told only
that Lazarus is sick, knows when he has died, and he waits an additional
two days so there is no doubt that he's dead when he arrives to resurrect
him. We're even told Jesus waited those two days because he loved
Martha and Mary!

Now Jesus loved Martha and her sister and Lazarus. So, when he
heard that Lazarus was ill, he stayed two days longer in the place
where he was. (John 11:5-6)

How could this be love? Wouldn't it be more loving to go sooner and
end their sadness? But in his divine wisdom, Jesus knows waiting is
the best way to love them because loving them best is showing them
God's glory. Only God can resurrect the dead, and only God can give
eternal life.

On the other hand, when Jesus first arrives, before going to the tomb in
love to reveal his glory, we see Jesus' humanness as well:

When Jesus saw her weeping, and the Jews who had come with her also
weeping, he was deeply moved in his spirit and greatly troubled. And
he said, "Where have you laid him?" They said to him, "Lord, come
and see." Jesus wept. (John 11:33-35)

What a beautiful and moving image: The eternal Son of God overcome
with emotion and weeping. Jesus looked at the suffering and sadness;
he saw Mary and Martha mourning for their brother; he saw the others

lamenting; and he was overcome with grief and mourned with them –
even knowing that he would soon do the miraculous and raise Lazarus.

What's interesting is that the word here translated "deeply moved" is
thought to be too soft of a translation by many biblical scholars who
understand the original ancient Greek of the New Testament. The word
translated "deeply moved" (which is used again in **11:38** as Jesus comes
to the tomb[216]) can be translated *indignant* or *angered*. Scholar R.C.
Sproul believes the word could better be translated as "irate,"[217] and
scholar D. A. Carson prefers the translation "outraged."[218] Thus, the big
question is, *If Jesus knew full well that he was going to resurrect Lazarus,
what was he outraged about?*

He was grieved and outraged by death, which sin brought into the
world. He was grieved and outraged by suffering and sadness and
hopelessness. He was grieved and outraged by what sin and death had
done to his good creation. D.A. Carson proposes Jesus was outraged
with "the sin, sickness, and death in this fallen world that wrecks so
much havoc and generates so much sorrow" and the hopelessness and
despair of those mourning Lazarus in the face of death.[219]

But we know how the story ends. Lazarus lived again. Jesus came to
declare war on sin, suffering, and death. He came to give eternal life so
we don't have to be despaired by death – so we don't even have to fear
death. Jesus came to restore his creation, which he created good but sin
has corrupted. He came so we could be free of sin and live forever with
him. This is good news.

---

[216] John 11:38: "Then Jesus, deeply moved again, came to the tomb."
[217] *John* (St. Andrew's Expositional Commentary) by R.C. Sproul
(Reformation Trust, 2009).
[218] *The Gospel of John* (Pillar New Testament Commentary) by D.A. Carson.
[219] *Same as footnote # 218.*

Who Jesus Ain't

And this is important: Christians don't worship a God who stays far off in the heavens, casting down judgment on us from afar. We worship a God who entered into our physical world, into the fallenness, into the messiness and mud and filth and blood and tears – into the suffering and evil and death. We worship a God who groaned in his spirit and wept and suffered with us. We worship a God who looked death in the eyes and walked straight at it, willingly being tortured and murdered to provide for us a way to escape his justified wrath.

In **Revelation 21**, we're given a glimpse of the restored creation, a place where the Savior who wept will wipe away every tear:

Then I saw a new heaven and a new earth, for the first heaven and the first earth had passed away, and the sea was no more. And I saw the holy city, new Jerusalem, coming down out of heaven from God, prepared as a bride adorned for her husband. And I heard a loud voice from the throne saying, "Behold, the dwelling place of God is with man. He will dwell with them, and they will be his people, and God himself will be with them as their God. He will wipe away every tear from their eyes, and death shall be no more, neither shall there be mourning, nor crying, nor pain anymore, for the former things have passed away." And he who was seated on the throne said, "Behold, I am making all things new." (Revelation 21:1-5)

It's a place where those who proclaim the God-man Jesus of Nazareth as their Lord and Savior, who have believed what he accomplished on the cross and have received this free gift, will spend forever with their Liberator.

In **John 11:25-26**, before bringing her brother back to life, Jesus presented Martha with a statement and a question, a statement and question I pass on to you:

Who Jesus Ain't

"I am the resurrection and the life. Whoever believes in me, though he die, yet shall he live, and everyone who lives and believes in me shall never die. Do you believe this?"

This question is a fitting way to end this book because it brings us right back to the introduction where I presented another question from Jesus. And your answer to this second question depends on how you answer the first: "Who do you say that I am?"

Acknowledgements

Thank you to my "editors" for their feedback and insight:

Sharon Vogel
Tim Nussbaumer
Christine DiSebastian

Cover designed by Christine DiSebastian

About the Author

Steve DiSebastian is an elder at Point Community Church in Somerset and North Brunswick, New Jersey and a Master of Divinity student at Southern Baptist Theological Seminary (NYC Extension). His blog, *God From the Machine,* explores theology and apologetics and sometimes *The Walking Dead* and Indiana Jones. He is the author of *Searching the Bible for Mother God: Examining the Teachings of the World Mission Society Church of God.* He also enjoys training in Brazilian Jiujitsu. Steve grew up in southern New Jersey, not far from Philadelphia, and has taught high school English for over 15 years in Paterson, NJ. Once an atheist, he became a Christian in 2005.

Read *God From the Machine* blog, including Steve's testimony:
godfromthemachineblog.wordpress.com

Follow *God From the Machine* on Facebook:
facebook.com/godfromthemachineblog

Follow Steve on Twitter: **@SteveDiSeb**

Learn more about **Point Community Church**:
pointcommunitychurch.org

52469556R00116

Made in the USA
Charleston, SC
14 February 2016